Cannabis Culture: State by State

TABLE OF CONTENTS

Chapter 1: California - The Birthplace of Legal Cannabis Culture

California has always been a trailblazer when it comes to cannabis reform and culture, and it continues to lead the way in the national conversation about legalization and cannabis consumption. Often referred to as the birthplace of legal cannabis, California's relationship with the plant is deeply rooted in the state's diverse social movements, innovative industries, and progressive policies.

From the counterculture movements of the 1960s to the medical marijuana revolution in the 1990s, California has long been at the forefront of cannabis advocacy. The passage of Proposition 215 in 1996 marked the first time medical cannabis was legalized in the United States, setting the stage for broader legalization efforts. In 2016, California voters passed Proposition 64, legalizing recreational cannabis for adults over 21, and the state has since developed one of the largest and most sophisticated cannabis markets in the world.

But what truly sets California apart is its unique cannabis culture—a vibrant mix of food, music, festivals, dispensaries, tourism, and social movements that have woven cannabis into the very fabric of the state's identity.

Cannabis and California's Food Scene

California's culinary landscape is as diverse as its people, and cannabis has found a natural home in this world of creativity and innovation. The state's emphasis on organic, farm-to-table cuisine aligns perfectly with the growing demand for cannabis-infused foods that emphasize quality and sustainability.

Cannabis-infused edibles have evolved far beyond the stereotypical pot brownies. Today, California is home to some of the most sophisticated cannabis edibles on the market. From infused olive oils to gourmet chocolates and artisanal gummies, the state's chefs and cannabis brands are leading the way in culinary innovation.

Cannabis-infused dining experiences are also becoming increasingly popular, particularly in cities like Los Angeles and San Francisco, where chefs collaborate with cannabis companies to create multi-course, farm-to-table dinners featuring locally sourced ingredients paired with cannabis. These curated dining experiences often feature low-dose cannabis to allow diners to savor the flavors without becoming overly intoxicated. The focus is on flavor, quality, and the way cannabis complements the dining experience.

In the heart of wine country, cannabis-infused wine tastings and cannabis pairings with gourmet meals have become a growing trend. Cannabis sommeliers are emerging, offering advice on how to pair specific strains with food, much like a traditional wine sommelier.

Music, Art, and Cannabis

California has long been a hub for music, art, and creative expression, and cannabis has always played a role in the state's vibrant arts scene. From the early days of the psychedelic rock movement in San Francisco's Haight-Ashbury to the hip-hop culture of Los Angeles, cannabis has been both an inspiration and a muse for countless artists.

Today, cannabis is more openly celebrated in California's music and art communities than ever before. Major music festivals like Coachella, Outside Lands, and Lightning in a Bottle have embraced cannabis culture, with cannabis lounges and consumption areas now common at many events. The emergence of cannabis-friendly music festivals has provided a new avenue for artists and musicians to explore their creative connections with the plant.

Cannabis-themed art shows and exhibitions are also becoming popular, with galleries showcasing works that explore the intersection of cannabis and creativity. In cities like Los Angeles and Oakland, cannabis lounges host live art performances, where local artists create while under the influence of cannabis, offering audiences a glimpse into how the plant enhances the creative process.

California's rich history of supporting art and music festivals has helped solidify cannabis' role as a cultural touchstone, with many artists openly discussing the influence cannabis has had on their work and its importance in their creative process.

Festivals and Cannabis Culture

California is home to some of the most iconic cannabis festivals in the world, drawing enthusiasts from across the globe. These events are not only celebrations of cannabis but also serve as platforms for education, activism, and community building.

One of the most well-known festivals is the Emerald Cup, held annually in Northern California's Mendocino County, a region known for its craft cannabis cultivation. The Emerald Cup is a celebration of organic, sun-grown cannabis and is often regarded as the most prestigious competition for cannabis cultivators. In addition to showcasing the best cannabis products, the festival also features live music, educational seminars, and panel discussions on the future of the cannabis industry.

Another popular event is High Times Cannabis Cup, which takes place in various cities throughout the state. The Cannabis Cup is both a competition and a festival, where attendees can sample products from top cannabis brands, vote on their favorites, and learn more about cannabis culture through exhibits and workshops.

Los Angeles and San Francisco also host smaller, more niche cannabis events, such as Cannabis-infused yoga retreats, health and wellness festivals, and local cannabis pop-up markets. These gatherings highlight California's holistic approach to cannabis, where the plant is seen as part of a broader lifestyle focused on wellness and sustainability.

The Dispensary Experience in California

California's dispensaries are as diverse as the state's population. From high-end, luxurious retail spaces to more relaxed, neighborhood shops, dispensaries in California cater to a wide range of consumers, from first-time users to seasoned cannabis connoisseurs.

Cities like Los Angeles, San Francisco, and Oakland are home to some of the most innovative dispensaries in the world. Retail experiences are carefully curated, offering consumers an environment that blends education, comfort, and luxury. Some dispensaries are designed with a boutique atmosphere, where cannabis is displayed like fine art, while others focus on community engagement, offering spaces where people can gather and learn about cannabis in a welcoming environment.

Many dispensaries also offer on-site consumption lounges, where customers can try products before purchasing or relax with friends in a social setting. These consumption lounges are redefining the way people experience cannabis, creating spaces where it can be enjoyed safely and responsibly.

Cannabis Tourism in California

California's cannabis tourism industry is booming, drawing visitors from across the country and the world to experience its vibrant cannabis culture. The state's diverse geography—ranging from beaches to mountains to vineyards—provides the perfect backdrop for cannabis-friendly experiences.

One of the most popular activities for cannabis tourists is taking part in cannabis farm tours. In regions like Mendocino, Humboldt, and Sonoma Counties, visitors can tour organic cannabis farms, meet the growers, and learn about the cultivation process from seed to harvest. These tours often include cannabis tastings and educational workshops on sustainable growing practices.

In cities like Los Angeles, cannabis tour buses take visitors on guided tours of the city's best dispensaries, cannabis-friendly art galleries, and consumption lounges. These tours offer a unique way to explore the city's cannabis scene while enjoying its rich cultural landmarks.

Cannabis yoga retreats, spa treatments featuring CBD-infused oils, and cannabis cooking classes are also popular among tourists looking for wellness-focused cannabis experiences.

Challenges and Opportunities in California's Cannabis Culture

Despite the incredible growth of California's cannabis industry and culture, the state still faces significant challenges. High taxes, strict regulations, and competition from the illicit market have made it difficult for some businesses, particularly small farmers and independent retailers, to thrive. The persistence of the black market continues to undermine the legal market, as consumers often seek cheaper, untaxed products.

However, the opportunities for growth are vast. As California continues to innovate, the state remains a global leader in cannabis, influencing trends and shaping the future of cannabis culture worldwide. New products such as cannabis-infused beverages, sustainable packaging solutions, and wellness-focused cannabis experiences are expected to drive further growth in the market.

Chapter 2: Colorado - Pioneering Recreational Cannabis

Colorado holds a special place in cannabis history as one of the first states to legalize recreational cannabis, setting the stage for a national shift in cannabis policy. The passage of Amendment 64 in 2012 not only marked a significant victory for cannabis advocates but also transformed Colorado into a global hub for cannabis culture and tourism. Colorado's embrace of cannabis goes beyond the legal framework—it has shaped the state's identity, becoming deeply ingrained in its lifestyle, festivals, cuisine, and outdoor activities.

Known for its stunning natural landscapes, including the Rocky Mountains and vast open plains, Colorado has seamlessly integrated cannabis into its adventurous and laid-back way of life. From cannabis-infused culinary experiences to events celebrating both cannabis and the outdoors, Colorado has become a destination for those looking to explore the relationship between nature, wellness, and cannabis.

Cannabis and Outdoor Adventure

Colorado's reputation for outdoor activities, including skiing, hiking, and mountain biking, has found a natural companion in cannabis. Cannabis has become an essential part of the state's outdoor culture, with many residents and tourists alike enjoying cannabis while taking in the natural beauty of the Rocky Mountains. From Denver to Boulder and Aspen, cannabis enthusiasts can be found partaking in outdoor adventures while incorporating cannabis into their experiences.

Several cannabis-friendly retreats and tours have sprung up across the state, offering visitors the chance to explore Colorado's rugged landscapes while also enjoying cannabis. These experiences often combine cannabis consumption with hiking, yoga, meditation, and even snowboarding, creating a holistic wellness experience in nature.

420-friendly campsites and mountain retreats offer cannabis enthusiasts the opportunity to unwind in nature while consuming cannabis responsibly. These campsites, located in picturesque settings, often feature cabins, tents, or RVs, allowing tourists to enjoy the great outdoors while partaking in cannabis.

Additionally, Colorado's ski towns, such as Aspen and Breckenridge, have embraced the cannabis culture, with dispensaries and cannabis consumption lounges catering to visitors looking to enhance their après-ski experience. Whether it's relaxing with a cannabis-infused hot cocoa after a day on the slopes or indulging in a cannabis-infused massage at a local spa, cannabis has become a key element of Colorado's outdoor lifestyle.

The Cannabis Dispensary Scene in Colorado

One of the most notable aspects of Colorado's cannabis culture is its thriving dispensary scene. Colorado was among the first states to develop a comprehensive legal framework for cannabis retail, and its dispensaries have since become models for other states looking to regulate cannabis sales.

In cities like Denver, Boulder, and Fort Collins, dispensaries range from sleek, high-end retail spaces to more laid-back, neighborhood shops. Many dispensaries take pride in offering a welcoming environment where customers can learn about cannabis, browse a wide variety of products, and enjoy personalized recommendations from knowledgeable budtenders.

Colorado's dispensaries offer an impressive selection of products, including flower, concentrates, edibles, topicals, and tinctures. The state is known for its high-quality cannabis products, and many dispensaries partner with local growers to source craft cannabis strains that are unique to Colorado. This commitment to quality has earned Colorado a reputation for producing some of the best cannabis in the country.

For visitors, dispensaries have become an essential stop on any cannabis tour of the state. Some dispensaries offer guided tours, where customers can learn about the cultivation and production processes, explore different product offerings, and gain insights into the science behind cannabis. These tours often end with a visit to a nearby consumption lounge, where customers can sample products in a relaxed setting.

In addition to traditional dispensaries, Colorado is home to several cannabis consumption lounges, where patrons can consume cannabis on-site. These lounges are designed to provide a safe and social environment for cannabis consumption, complete with comfortable seating, games, and live music. Consumption lounges are particularly popular in cities like Denver, where cannabis tourism is a major draw.

Cannabis Tourism in Colorado

Colorado's decision to legalize recreational cannabis has had a profound impact on its tourism industry. Since legalization, the state has become a top destination for cannabis enthusiasts, with cannabis tourism accounting for a significant portion of the state's overall tourism revenue.

Cannabis tourists flock to Colorado for a variety of experiences, from cannabis farm tours and dispensary visits to cannabis-friendly hotel stays and outdoor excursions. Many hotels and resorts offer cannabis-friendly accommodations, where guests can enjoy cannabis in designated areas or participate in cannabis-infused spa treatments.

One of the most popular activities for cannabis tourists is the cannabis tour bus experience, which takes visitors on a guided tour of the state's best dispensaries, cultivation facilities, and cannabis-friendly venues. These tours provide a comprehensive look at Colorado's cannabis industry, from seed to sale, and often include educational workshops on topics such as cannabis cultivation, edibles, and responsible consumption.

In cities like Denver and Boulder, cannabis cooking classes have become a popular attraction, allowing visitors to learn how to create gourmet cannabis-infused meals. These classes are led by professional chefs who teach participants how to infuse oils, butter, and other ingredients with cannabis, creating delicious and sophisticated dishes that elevate the culinary experience.

Additionally, Colorado's cannabis yoga retreats have gained popularity, combining cannabis consumption with wellness practices such as yoga, meditation, and mindfulness. These retreats are often held in scenic locations, such as mountain resorts or nature lodges, and offer participants the chance to relax, recharge, and connect with nature while enjoying cannabis.

Cannabis Festivals and Events in Colorado

Colorado's cannabis festivals are some of the most well-known in the world, attracting thousands of attendees from across the globe. These festivals celebrate cannabis culture in all its forms, from music and art to education and advocacy.

One of the most famous festivals is the annual 420 Fest held in Denver. This event, which takes place on April 20th each year, is a massive celebration of cannabis, featuring live music, food vendors, and cannabis-related activities. Thousands of people gather at Denver's Civic Center Park to celebrate cannabis and advocate for its continued legalization. The festival is a symbol of Colorado's commitment to cannabis freedom and is one of the largest cannabis events in the United States.

Another major event is the Mile High Cannabis Festival, which showcases the best of Colorado's cannabis industry. This festival brings together cannabis businesses, consumers, and advocates for a weekend of networking, education, and entertainment. Attendees can explore vendor booths, sample products, and attend workshops on topics such as cannabis law, cultivation, and entrepreneurship.

Colorado is also home to the Indo Expo, one of the largest cannabis trade shows in the country. This event brings together industry professionals, cultivators, and cannabis enthusiasts for a weekend of exhibits, panels, and networking opportunities. The Indo Expo is a major event for those looking to learn more about the cannabis industry and stay up-to-date on the latest trends and innovations.

Cannabis Cuisine in Colorado

Colorado has embraced cannabis-infused cuisine, with a growing number of restaurants and chefs incorporating cannabis into their menus. The state's cannabis-infused dining scene is diverse, offering everything from casual edibles to gourmet multi-course meals.

Many of Colorado's cannabis-infused dishes focus on highlighting local ingredients, with an emphasis on farm-to-table dining. Cannabis-infused farm dinners have become particularly popular, where guests are treated to multi-course meals featuring locally sourced ingredients paired with cannabis. These dinners often take place in scenic outdoor locations, such as organic farms or vineyards, and provide a relaxed, communal dining experience.

Colorado's cannabis-infused beverages are also making waves, with companies creating everything from THC-infused sodas and sparkling waters to cannabis cocktails. These beverages provide a convenient and discreet way for consumers to enjoy cannabis, offering an alternative to smoking or vaping.

The state's cannabis cafes and pop-up restaurants are also gaining popularity, offering a social dining experience where cannabis is an integral part of the meal. At these events, guests can sample a variety of cannabis-infused dishes, from appetizers to desserts, while enjoying live music, art, and entertainment.

Challenges and Opportunities in Colorado's Cannabis Market

While Colorado has enjoyed immense success as a pioneer in cannabis legalization, the state's cannabis industry faces several challenges. One of the biggest hurdles is the high taxation on cannabis products, which can drive consumers to the illicit market in search of cheaper alternatives. Additionally, the strict regulations around advertising and packaging have made it difficult for businesses to reach new customers.

Despite these challenges, the opportunities for growth in Colorado's cannabis market are vast. As the state continues to innovate in areas such as sustainable cultivation, cannabis tourism, and product development, Colorado remains at the forefront of the national cannabis industry. The state's commitment to social equity, consumer safety, and community engagement will ensure that it continues to be a leader in cannabis culture for years to come.

Chapter 3: Oregon - A Hub for Craft Cannabis and Sustainability

Oregon has earned its reputation as one of the most progressive states in the United States, and its cannabis culture is no exception. With a long history of cannabis activism, medical legalization, and, eventually, full recreational legalization, Oregon has built a cannabis industry that reflects the state's values of sustainability, craftsmanship, and community. Oregon's cannabis culture thrives on small-batch cultivation, organic practices, and a deep connection to the environment, making it a unique hub for cannabis enthusiasts seeking quality over quantity.

From the lush greenery of the Willamette Valley to the craft-focused cities of Portland and Eugene, Oregon's cannabis scene embraces a holistic approach that includes organic farming practices, eco-conscious packaging, and a commitment to local, artisanal products. The state's focus on sustainability is matched by its vibrant community of artists, musicians, and activists who have helped shape Oregon's cannabis identity.

Craft Cannabis: The Heart of Oregon's Industry

At the core of Oregon's cannabis culture is its dedication to craft cannabis. Unlike other states where large-scale commercial operations dominate the market, Oregon has made room for smaller, independent growers who focus on producing high-quality, small-batch cannabis. These growers often use sustainable farming methods, including organic soil cultivation, minimal water usage, and pesticide-free growing practices.

Many of Oregon's craft cannabis producers are located in rural areas, such as Southern Oregon and the Willamette Valley, where the mild climate and fertile soil provide ideal growing conditions for cannabis. These growers take pride in their artisanal approach, carefully selecting strains that reflect the unique terroir of their farms. This connection to the land is a fundamental part of Oregon's cannabis culture, with many cultivators viewing cannabis not just as a product, but as a way to connect with nature.

Sungrown cannabis is particularly popular in Oregon, with many farms opting to grow their plants outdoors using only natural sunlight. Sungrown cannabis is often seen as a more sustainable alternative to indoor growing, which requires significant amounts of energy for lighting and climate control. Oregon's climate, with its long, sunny summers and cool, wet winters, is ideal for outdoor cannabis cultivation, and many of the state's growers take advantage of these natural conditions to produce high-quality, environmentally friendly cannabis.

Oregon's commitment to sustainability extends beyond cultivation. Many dispensaries in the state prioritize eco-friendly packaging, using materials that are recyclable, compostable, or biodegradable. This focus on sustainability is part of a broader movement in Oregon to reduce the environmental impact of the cannabis industry, making it a model for other states looking to create a more sustainable cannabis market.

The Dispensary Experience in Oregon

Oregon's dispensaries reflect the state's emphasis on craftsmanship and community. While there are larger chain dispensaries, many of the most popular shops are independently owned and operated, offering a more personal, boutique experience. These dispensaries are often designed with a focus on creating a welcoming and educational atmosphere, where customers can learn about cannabis and explore a wide variety of products.

In cities like Portland and Eugene, dispensaries are as diverse as the consumers they serve. Some cater to the wellness crowd, offering CBD-rich products and cannabis-infused health and beauty items, while others focus on more recreational products like edibles, concentrates, and flower. Many dispensaries partner with local growers and producers to offer a curated selection of Oregon's best craft cannabis, ensuring that customers have access to the highest quality products available.

One of the unique aspects of Oregon's dispensary scene is the focus on education. Budtenders are often highly knowledgeable about cannabis and are eager to help customers find products that meet their specific needs, whether it's for pain relief, relaxation, or enhancing creativity. Many dispensaries also host educational events, such as Cannabis 101 classes and strain tastings, where customers can learn more about the different types of cannabis and how they interact with the body.

For those looking for a more relaxed shopping experience, cannabis cafes and lounges have started to pop up in Oregon, providing a space where people can consume cannabis in a social setting. These cafes often feature comfortable seating, live music, and a menu of cannabis-infused food and drinks, creating a laid-back environment for consumers to enjoy their products.

Oregon's Cannabis Festivals and Events

Oregon's cannabis festivals and events celebrate the state's love for craft cannabis, sustainability, and community. These gatherings offer an opportunity for cannabis enthusiasts, cultivators, and industry professionals to come together and share their passion for the plant.

One of the most well-known festivals in Oregon is the Oregon Cannabis Festival, held annually in Portland. This event brings together cannabis consumers, growers, and advocates for a weekend of live music, educational seminars, and cannabis tastings. The festival also features a cannabis competition, where local growers can showcase their best strains, edibles, and concentrates, competing for awards in categories such as potency, flavor, and appearance.

Another popular event is the Hemp and Cannabis Fair, which takes place in multiple cities across Oregon, including Eugene and Medford. This traveling festival focuses on education and advocacy, offering workshops on topics like growing techniques, cannabis law, and wellness applications. The fair also includes vendor booths, where attendees can sample products from local dispensaries and cannabis companies.

For those interested in exploring the connection between cannabis and the environment, Oregon is home to several cannabis-friendly wellness retreats. These retreats often combine cannabis consumption with outdoor activities like hiking, yoga, and meditation, allowing participants to connect with nature while exploring the benefits of cannabis. These retreats are popular among visitors looking to experience Oregon's natural beauty while incorporating cannabis into their wellness routine.

Cannabis and Oregon's Food Culture

Oregon's food scene is renowned for its focus on fresh, locally sourced ingredients, and cannabis has found its way into the state's culinary landscape. In cities like Portland, chefs and cannabis producers have teamed up to create unique cannabis-infused dining experiences that highlight the state's agricultural bounty.

One of the most popular forms of cannabis cuisine in Oregon is the infused dinner. These multi-course meals, often held at private venues or pop-up restaurants, feature dishes infused with cannabis in various forms, such as THC-infused oils or CBD-rich sauces. The meals are designed to provide a subtle cannabis experience, with low doses that enhance the flavor of the food without overwhelming the diner. Many of these dinners also feature local wines and craft beers, creating a full sensory experience that highlights Oregon's culinary and cannabis cultures.

Cannabis-infused edibles are also a major part of Oregon's cannabis market. Local producers offer a wide range of artisanal edibles, including chocolates, gummies, baked goods, and beverages. Many of these products are made with organic, locally sourced ingredients, reflecting Oregon's commitment to sustainability and quality.

In addition to infused foods, Oregon is home to several cannabis-friendly breweries and distilleries that offer THC-infused beverages. These beverages provide a unique way to enjoy cannabis, offering a social alternative to smoking or vaping. Many of these breweries and distilleries partner with local cannabis growers to create custom-infused drinks that reflect the flavors and terroir of Oregon's cannabis.

Cannabis Tourism in Oregon

Oregon has become a top destination for cannabis tourism, attracting visitors from across the country and around the world. The state's relaxed approach to cannabis, combined with its stunning natural landscapes and vibrant cities, makes it an ideal location for those looking to experience cannabis in a welcoming and scenic environment.

One of the most popular activities for cannabis tourists is the cannabis farm tour. Oregon's rural areas, particularly in Southern Oregon, are home to numerous cannabis farms that offer guided tours where visitors can learn about the cultivation process, meet the growers, and sample fresh cannabis products. These tours often include educational workshops on sustainable growing practices, as well as opportunities to purchase cannabis directly from the farm.

For those looking to combine cannabis with outdoor adventure, Oregon offers cannabis-friendly camping and yoga retreats. These retreats provide a space where visitors can consume cannabis while enjoying activities like hiking, meditation, and wellness workshops. Many of these retreats are located in scenic areas, such as the Oregon Coast or the Cascade Mountains, providing a serene backdrop for relaxation and reflection.

In cities like Portland, cannabis tourists can explore cannabis tours that take them to some of the city's best dispensaries, lounges, and cannabis-friendly cafes. These tours offer a curated experience, allowing visitors to learn about Oregon's cannabis industry while sampling products from top producers.

Challenges and Opportunities in Oregon's Cannabis Market

Oregon's cannabis industry has seen tremendous growth since legalization, but it has also faced challenges, particularly in terms of oversupply. The state's fertile growing conditions and abundance of licensed growers have led to a surplus of cannabis, driving down prices and making it difficult for some producers to stay competitive. This oversupply has also contributed to the persistence of the black market, as some growers seek to sell their excess product outside of the regulated market.

Despite these challenges, Oregon's cannabis industry remains resilient, with opportunities for growth in areas such as cannabis tourism, sustainability, and craft cannabis. As consumers continue to demand high-quality, locally sourced products, Oregon's focus on craftsmanship and environmental responsibility positions it as a leader in the national cannabis market.

As the state continues to innovate, Oregon's cannabis culture will likely evolve, with new opportunities for entrepreneurs, growers, and consumers alike. Whether through the development of new products, the expansion of cannabis tourism, or the continued focus on sustainability, Oregon's cannabis scene will remain a key player in shaping the future of cannabis in the United States.

Chapter 4: Washington - Progressive Cannabis Culture in the Pacific Northwest

Washington is one of the pioneers of cannabis reform in the United States, and its progressive cannabis culture reflects the spirit of innovation and activism that the Pacific Northwest is known for. As the second state to legalize recreational cannabis, following Colorado, Washington set the stage for the rest of the nation to follow. The state's rich cannabis culture is deeply intertwined with its music scene, its eco-conscious mindset, and its diverse urban and rural communities.

From the bustling streets of Seattle to the quiet, green expanses of rural Washington, the state has embraced cannabis in ways that reflect its unique character. With a thriving dispensary scene, innovative cannabis festivals, and a growing cannabis tourism industry, Washington has solidified itself as a major player in the cannabis movement.

Cannabis and Seattle's Creative Scene

Seattle has long been a hub for creativity and innovation, and cannabis has been a central part of that scene for decades. Known for its rich music history—particularly the rise of grunge in the early 1990s—Seattle has always had a deep connection to alternative lifestyles and counterculture. Cannabis has played an important role in shaping the city's music, art, and cultural identity.

The city's famous music venues, such as The Crocodile and Neumos, have hosted countless legendary performances where cannabis was a common part of the audience's experience. Today, cannabis remains an integral part of Seattle's creative community, with musicians, artists, and performers openly celebrating its influence on their work.

Seattle is also home to a growing number of cannabis-friendly art shows and live music events, where cannabis consumption is encouraged in a social and creative setting. These events often feature live art installations, interactive performances, and cannabis-infused food and drinks, offering attendees a chance to experience cannabis in a way that enhances their creativity and connection to the arts.

For visitors and locals alike, cannabis consumption lounges in Seattle are increasingly becoming popular venues for enjoying cannabis while engaging in the city's rich artistic culture. These lounges provide comfortable, stylish environments where people can consume cannabis in a social setting, often while enjoying live music, art exhibits, and interactive experiences.

Washington's Dispensary Scene

Washington's dispensary scene is one of the most well-established in the country, having transitioned from a thriving medical cannabis market to a robust recreational market. Dispensaries in Washington range from sleek, high-end retail spaces in Seattle to more rustic, community-oriented shops in the state's rural areas.

One of the unique aspects of Washington's dispensary culture is its emphasis on customer education. Many dispensaries offer a wide range of resources for new and experienced consumers alike, including product guides, strain recommendations, and information on dosing. Budtenders are highly knowledgeable and are often trained to help customers find the products that best suit their needs, whether for medical or recreational use.

In Seattle, dispensaries like The Green Room and Dockside Cannabis have become well-known for their commitment to high-quality products and customer service. These dispensaries often feature modern, minimalist designs, creating a clean and welcoming environment for customers to browse and shop. Many dispensaries in Washington also partner with local cannabis growers to offer artisan strains that are unique to the region.

For those interested in exploring Washington's cannabis culture beyond the city, dispensaries in rural areas offer a more personal and laid-back experience. Dispensaries in towns like Olympia, Bellingham, and Spokane often serve as community hubs, where locals gather to learn about cannabis, attend workshops, and participate in events.

Additionally, Washington is home to a growing number of delivery services that cater to customers who prefer to shop from the comfort of their own homes. These services allow customers to order cannabis online and have it delivered directly to their door, making it easier than ever to access high-quality cannabis products.

Cannabis and Sustainability in Washington

Washington's cannabis industry has embraced the state's strong commitment to environmental sustainability. Many of the state's growers and producers prioritize eco-friendly practices, such as organic farming methods, water conservation, and the use of renewable energy.

One of the most notable trends in Washington's cannabis market is the rise of sungrown cannabis. Like neighboring Oregon, Washington's climate is well-suited for outdoor cannabis cultivation, and many of the state's growers take advantage of the natural sunlight to produce high-quality cannabis while minimizing their environmental impact. Sungrown cannabis is often seen as a more sustainable alternative to indoor growing, which requires significant energy for lighting and climate control.

In addition to sustainable cultivation practices, Washington's cannabis industry has made strides in reducing the environmental impact of packaging. Dispensaries and producers are increasingly opting for eco-friendly packaging options, such as compostable and recyclable materials.

In keeping with Washington's focus on craft cannabis, many dispensaries prioritize sourcing their products from local growers who use organic and sustainable farming practices. This emphasis on locally sourced, high-quality cannabis reflects the state's broader commitment to environmental stewardship and social responsibility.

In addition to traditional dispensaries, Washington has embraced cannabis lounges, where customers can consume cannabis in a safe and social environment. These lounges often feature comfortable seating, board games, and even live performances, creating a space where cannabis users can relax, socialize, and enjoy cannabis in a legal setting. Seattle, in particular, has become a hub for these types of venues, attracting both locals and tourists who want to experience the state's unique cannabis culture.

Washington's dispensaries also offer a wide variety of products, from flower and concentrates to edibles and topicals. The state is known for its high standards in product testing, ensuring that all products sold in dispensaries meet strict safety and quality standards. Many dispensaries work closely with local cultivators to offer exclusive, small-batch strains that are unique to the region, giving Washington's cannabis consumers access to some of the finest cannabis available in the country.

Cannabis Festivals and Events in Washington

Washington is home to a number of high-profile cannabis festivals and events that celebrate the state's progressive approach to cannabis and its cultural significance. These events provide a platform for cannabis enthusiasts, industry professionals, and advocates to come together, share knowledge, and celebrate cannabis culture.

One of the most famous cannabis events in Washington is Hempfest, an annual festival held in Seattle that has been a cornerstone of cannabis activism since its inception in 1991. Hempfest is a massive celebration of cannabis culture, drawing tens of thousands of attendees each year. The festival features live music, keynote speakers, vendor booths, and educational workshops on everything from cannabis cultivation to legal advocacy. Hempfest is not only a celebration of cannabis but also a call to action for continued cannabis reform, making it one of the most important cannabis events in the country.

Another major event is CannaCon, a cannabis industry expo that takes place annually in Seattle. CannaCon brings together cannabis businesses, entrepreneurs, and consumers for a weekend of networking, product showcases, and educational panels. The event is a must-attend for anyone involved in the cannabis industry, offering insights into the latest trends, technologies, and innovations shaping the future of cannabis.

For those interested in more niche events, Washington hosts a variety of cannabis-friendly art shows, yoga classes, and wellness retreats that integrate cannabis consumption with creative and healing practices. These events often take place in smaller, more intimate settings, allowing participants to explore the relationship between cannabis and personal well-being in a relaxed and supportive environment.

Washington's Cannabis and Food Scene

Washington's food scene, particularly in cities like Seattle, has embraced cannabis as part of its innovative and adventurous approach to cuisine. The state is known for its focus on fresh, locally sourced ingredients, and cannabis-infused dishes are no exception. Cannabis-infused dining experiences have become a popular attraction in Washington, with chefs and cannabis producers collaborating to create gourmet meals that incorporate cannabis into each course.

These multi-course dinners are often held in private venues or pop-up restaurants, offering a sophisticated dining experience that highlights the flavors of the Pacific Northwest while incorporating cannabis in subtle, well-balanced ways. Each course is paired with a different strain or infused ingredient, allowing diners to experience the full spectrum of cannabis' culinary potential. These meals typically feature low doses of THC, ensuring that diners can enjoy the effects of cannabis without becoming overly intoxicated.

In addition to cannabis-infused dinners, Washington is home to a growing number of cannabis-friendly cafes and bakeries that offer a variety of edibles, from cookies and brownies to infused teas and coffees. These cafes provide a casual setting where customers can enjoy cannabis-infused treats while socializing with friends or working remotely.

Washington's cannabis beverage market is also on the rise, with local producers creating a variety of THC-infused sodas, tonics, and sparkling waters. These beverages provide a discreet and convenient way to consume cannabis, offering a refreshing alternative to traditional edibles or smoking. Many of these beverages are produced by small, independent companies that prioritize sustainability and local sourcing, reflecting Washington's commitment to both quality and environmental responsibility.

Cannabis Tourism in Washington

Washington's cannabis tourism industry has grown steadily since the legalization of recreational cannabis, drawing visitors from across the country and around the world. The state's diverse landscapes, from the urban bustle of Seattle to the serene beauty of the Olympic Peninsula, make it an ideal destination for cannabis tourists seeking both adventure and relaxation.

Cannabis tours have become a popular attraction in Washington, offering visitors the chance to explore the state's cannabis industry while learning about the cultivation, production, and distribution of cannabis. These tours often include visits to dispensaries, grow facilities, and consumption lounges, giving tourists an insider's look at Washington's cannabis culture. In Seattle, some cannabis tour companies even offer 420-friendly cruises on the Puget Sound, where guests can consume cannabis while taking in the stunning views of the city's skyline and surrounding mountains.

For those looking to combine cannabis with outdoor activities, Washington offers a variety of cannabis-friendly retreats that cater to wellness and relaxation. These retreats often take place in scenic locations, such as the San Juan Islands or the Cascade Mountains, and feature activities like yoga, hiking, and meditation. Participants can enjoy cannabis in a serene and natural setting, allowing them to connect with both the plant and their surroundings.

In addition to wellness retreats, Washington is home to several cannabis-friendly hotels and lodges that cater to cannabis consumers. These accommodations offer designated consumption areas, cannabis-infused spa treatments, and guided tours of nearby cannabis attractions, making them a popular choice for tourists looking to experience Washington's cannabis culture in a comfortable and welcoming environment.

Challenges and Opportunities in Washington's Cannabis Market

While Washington's cannabis industry has enjoyed significant success since legalization, it has also faced its share of challenges. One of the biggest issues is high taxation, which can make legal cannabis products more expensive than those available on the black market. This has led to concerns about the long-term sustainability of the legal market, particularly for smaller businesses that struggle to compete with illicit operators.

Another challenge is regulatory compliance, as Washington has some of the strictest cannabis regulations in the country. Dispensaries and producers must adhere to rigorous testing and labeling requirements, which can be costly and time-consuming. While these regulations are intended to ensure consumer safety, they have also created barriers for small businesses trying to enter the market.

Despite these challenges, Washington's cannabis industry continues to thrive, with opportunities for growth in areas like sustainability, product innovation, and cannabis tourism. As the state continues to refine its regulatory framework and explore new market opportunities, Washington remains a leader in both the national and global cannabis landscapes.

Chapter 5: Nevada - Cannabis and the Entertainment Capital

Nevada's foray into the cannabis industry has been nothing short of transformative, with Las Vegas leading the charge in integrating cannabis into its already bustling entertainment scene. Known worldwide as the Entertainment Capital of the World, Las Vegas has quickly become a destination for cannabis enthusiasts looking to combine their love of cannabis with the vibrant nightlife, luxury experiences, and unique attractions the city has to offer. Since the legalization of recreational cannabis in 2016, Nevada has embraced cannabis not just as a product but as an integral part of the state's tourism and entertainment industry.

Beyond the bright lights of the Las Vegas Strip, cannabis culture has spread throughout Nevada, influencing food, music, events, and retail experiences across the state. The combination of high-end luxury and accessibility has made Nevada's cannabis industry one of the most dynamic and fast-growing in the country.

The Rise of Cannabis Dispensaries in Nevada

Nevada's dispensary scene is a reflection of the state's unique blend of luxury and accessibility. From the sleek, high-end dispensaries that cater to tourists along the Las Vegas Strip to more relaxed, community-oriented shops in Reno, Nevada offers a variety of retail experiences to meet the needs of its diverse customer base. The state's cannabis regulations require strict compliance with licensing, security, and quality control, ensuring that all products sold in dispensaries are safe, tested, and of high quality.

Many of Nevada's dispensaries, particularly those in Las Vegas, have taken the retail experience to the next level by offering luxurious, immersive environments where customers can explore products in a setting that rivals the finest boutiques. These dispensaries often feature sleek, modern designs, personalized service from knowledgeable budtenders, and an extensive selection of products ranging from premium flower and concentrates to high-end edibles and topicals.

One of the standout dispensaries in Las Vegas is Planet 13, which is not only the largest cannabis dispensary in Nevada but also one of the largest in the world. Spanning over 100,000 square feet, Planet 13 offers visitors a one-of-a-kind cannabis shopping experience that includes interactive displays, a full-service coffee shop, and a viewing area where customers can watch cannabis products being made in real-time. The dispensary also features a cannabis-infused restaurant, where guests can enjoy gourmet meals while sampling a variety of cannabis products.

Other notable dispensaries in Las Vegas include The Apothecary Shoppe and Essence Cannabis Dispensary, both of which offer a high-end retail experience with a focus on premium products and personalized customer service. These dispensaries cater to tourists looking for an upscale cannabis experience, complete with concierge-level service and curated product selections.

Cannabis and Nevada's Entertainment Industry

Cannabis has quickly become a major part of Nevada's entertainment industry, particularly in Las Vegas, where the city's reputation for indulgence and excess has made it the perfect destination for cannabis-friendly experiences. From cannabis-infused events to consumption lounges, Nevada is exploring new ways to integrate cannabis into its world-famous nightlife and entertainment scene.

One of the most exciting developments in Nevada's cannabis culture is the rise of cannabis consumption lounges, where visitors can legally consume cannabis in a social setting. These lounges are expected to become a major draw for tourists, offering a safe and comfortable environment for cannabis consumption without the risk of violating hotel or public consumption laws. While consumption lounges were legalized in 2021, the state is still in the process of developing regulations for these spaces, but many believe they will soon become a staple of the Las Vegas entertainment experience.

Cannabis-themed events have also become a popular attraction in Nevada, with many festivals and conventions incorporating cannabis into their programming. One of the most well-known events is the Las Vegas Cannabis Awards, which celebrates the best in the cannabis industry, from top dispensaries and brands to influential cannabis advocates and entrepreneurs. The event features live performances, award ceremonies, and plenty of opportunities for networking and sampling products.

In addition to cannabis awards shows, cannabis music festivals are gaining popularity in Nevada. These festivals feature performances by top artists, vendor booths from leading cannabis brands, and designated consumption areas where attendees can legally enjoy cannabis. Events like these have helped solidify Las Vegas as a destination for cannabis enthusiasts who want to combine their love of music and cannabis in a high-energy environment.

Cannabis Tourism in Nevada

Tourism is one of Nevada's largest industries, and cannabis has quickly become a key part of the tourism experience, especially in Las Vegas. The city's status as a global destination for entertainment, combined with its legalization of recreational cannabis, has made it a magnet for cannabis tourists seeking a unique and luxurious cannabis experience.

One of the most popular activities for cannabis tourists is the cannabis tour bus, which takes visitors on a guided tour of some of Las Vegas' best dispensaries, consumption lounges, and cannabis-related attractions. These tours often include behind-the-scenes access to cultivation facilities, where guests can learn about the cannabis growing process, as well as stops at some of the city's most iconic landmarks.

For those looking for a more immersive experience, several cannabis-friendly hotels in Las Vegas offer accommodations that cater specifically to cannabis consumers. These hotels provide designated smoking areas, cannabis-infused room service, and even curated cannabis experiences that allow guests to explore the city's cannabis scene without leaving their hotel.

Nevada's cannabis tourism isn't limited to Las Vegas, either. In Northern Nevada, cities like Reno and Lake Tahoe are also embracing cannabis culture, with dispensaries offering cannabis-infused spa treatments, cannabis-friendly cabins in the mountains, and cannabis yoga retreats. These experiences allow tourists to enjoy the natural beauty of Nevada while incorporating cannabis into their relaxation and wellness routines.

Cannabis-Infused Cuisine in Nevada

Nevada's culinary scene has always been a major draw for tourists, and cannabis-infused cuisine is becoming an increasingly popular part of the state's food culture. In Las Vegas, several high-end restaurants and chefs are experimenting with cannabis-infused dishes, offering guests the chance to enjoy gourmet meals paired with cannabis.

Cannabis-infused dining experiences in Las Vegas range from casual pop-up dinners to multi-course meals prepared by celebrity chefs. These meals often feature dishes infused with low doses of THC or CBD, allowing diners to experience the effects of cannabis in a subtle and controlled way. The focus is on flavor and presentation, with chefs using cannabis as an ingredient to enhance the overall dining experience rather than as the main attraction.

One of the most exciting developments in the world of cannabis cuisine is the rise of cannabis-infused cocktails. Several bars and lounges in Las Vegas are now offering THC or CBD-infused cocktails, providing a unique twist on classic drinks. These cannabis cocktails are often made with fresh, locally sourced ingredients and are designed to offer a refreshing, non-alcoholic alternative for those looking to enjoy cannabis in a social setting.

For those who prefer a more casual cannabis dining experience, Nevada's dispensaries offer a wide range of edibles, including chocolates, gummies, cookies, and more. These products are perfect for tourists who want to enjoy cannabis discreetly while exploring the city, and many dispensaries offer edibles that are specifically designed for microdosing, allowing consumers to enjoy the effects of cannabis without becoming overly intoxicated.

Challenges and Opportunities in Nevada's Cannabis Industry

Nevada's cannabis industry has experienced rapid growth since the legalization of recreational cannabis, but it has also faced several challenges, particularly in terms of regulatory compliance and taxation. The state's strict regulations around cannabis advertising, packaging, and testing have made it difficult for some businesses to operate, particularly smaller companies that may not have the resources to meet these requirements.

High taxes on cannabis products have also been a point of contention, with some consumers opting to purchase from the black market to avoid paying the premium prices associated with legal cannabis. Despite these challenges, Nevada's cannabis industry continues to thrive, with dispensaries, lounges, and cannabis-related events attracting both locals and tourists.

One of the most exciting opportunities for growth in Nevada's cannabis market is the development of cannabis consumption lounges. These lounges are expected to become a major draw for tourists, offering a safe and legal space for cannabis consumption that aligns with Nevada's reputation as a destination for luxury and indulgence. As regulations around these lounges are finalized, many in the industry believe they will help cement Nevada's status as one of the top cannabis destinations in the world.

Nevada's cannabis industry also has the potential to lead in the area of cannabis hospitality, with hotels, resorts, and spas offering unique cannabis experiences that cater to a wide range of consumers. Whether through cannabis-infused spa treatments, cannabis-friendly rooms, or curated cannabis tours, the state has the opportunity to redefine what cannabis tourism looks like on a global scale.

Chapter 6: Michigan - The Midwest's Booming Cannabis Market

Michigan has emerged as a powerhouse in the cannabis industry, becoming the first state in the Midwest to legalize recreational cannabis in 2018. The state's progressive approach to cannabis reform has placed it at the forefront of the cannabis movement in the region, offering a model for other Midwestern states looking to embrace legalization. From Detroit's urban cannabis scene to small-town growers, Michigan's cannabis industry is booming, and the state is quickly becoming a hub for cannabis culture in the Midwest.

Michigan's cannabis culture reflects the state's diverse population and its rich history of activism, craftsmanship, and innovation. The state has a thriving medical cannabis program, and with recreational legalization, Michigan has seen rapid growth in both the number of dispensaries and cannabis-related events. From cannabis festivals and food to music and art, Michigan's cannabis culture is deeply ingrained in its local communities, making it a unique and vibrant market.

The Evolution of Michigan's Cannabis Industry

Michigan's journey toward cannabis legalization began with the passage of the Michigan Medical Marihuana Act in 2008. This law allowed patients with qualifying medical conditions to use cannabis under the supervision of a physician. The state's medical cannabis program grew steadily over the years, laying the groundwork for the eventual legalization of recreational cannabis.

In 2018, Michigan voters approved Proposal 1, which legalized recreational cannabis for adults over the age of 21. This marked a major turning point for the state, as it became the first in the Midwest to establish a legal recreational cannabis market. The state quickly developed a regulatory framework for licensing dispensaries, growers, and processors, and legal sales began in December 2019.

Since then, Michigan's cannabis industry has experienced rapid growth. The state is now home to hundreds of dispensaries, cultivation facilities, and cannabis-related businesses. Michigan's cannabis market is one of the largest in the country, generating significant tax revenue and creating thousands of jobs. The state's thriving cannabis scene has also attracted entrepreneurs, investors, and tourists from across the country.

The Dispensary Experience in Michigan

Michigan's dispensaries offer a diverse range of experiences, from high-end retail spaces in urban areas to small, locally owned shops in rural communities. Dispensaries in cities like Detroit, Ann Arbor, and Grand Rapids cater to a wide range of consumers, from medical patients seeking relief to recreational users looking for premium products.

Detroit, in particular, has become a hub for the state's cannabis industry. The city is home to some of the state's largest and most well-known dispensaries, many of which offer a luxurious, boutique-style shopping experience. These dispensaries often feature sleek, modern designs, knowledgeable budtenders, and a curated selection of cannabis products, including flower, concentrates, edibles, and topicals. Many also offer delivery services, making it easier for customers to access their products.

Outside of the major cities, Michigan's smaller towns have also embraced cannabis culture, with locally owned dispensaries offering a more intimate, community-focused experience. These shops often pride themselves on supporting local growers and producers, offering products that are unique to the region. In many cases, the budtenders are also growers or have close relationships with local cultivators, giving them a deep knowledge of the products they sell.

One of the unique aspects of Michigan's cannabis industry is its focus on craft cannabis. Many of the state's dispensaries partner with local, small-batch growers who use organic and sustainable farming practices. This focus on craftsmanship and quality has helped differentiate Michigan's cannabis market from other states, with consumers showing a strong preference for locally sourced, artisanal products.

Cannabis Festivals and Events in Michigan

Michigan's cannabis festivals and events play a key role in the state's cannabis culture, providing a platform for enthusiasts, businesses, and advocates to come together and celebrate the plant. These events often feature live music, educational workshops, vendor booths, and opportunities for networking and community building.

One of the most famous cannabis events in Michigan is the Ann Arbor Hash Bash, which has been held annually since 1972. Hash Bash is a celebration of cannabis culture and activism, attracting thousands of attendees each year. The event includes speeches from cannabis advocates, live music, and a vendor village where attendees can purchase products from local businesses. Hash Bash is more than just a festival—it is a symbol of Michigan's long-standing commitment to cannabis reform and social justice.

Another major event is the Cannabis Cup, which takes place in Detroit and brings together some of the best cannabis producers and brands from across the state. The Cannabis Cup is both a competition and a festival, where attendees can sample products, vote on their favorites, and learn more about the latest trends in the cannabis industry. The event also features live performances, educational panels, and opportunities to network with industry professionals.

In addition to these larger events, Michigan is home to numerous smaller cannabis festivals, pop-up markets, and educational workshops. Many of these events focus on topics such as cultivation techniques, cannabis law, and wellness applications, providing valuable resources for both consumers and industry professionals.

Cannabis and Michigan's Food Culture

Michigan's food scene has embraced cannabis in a big way, with chefs and producers experimenting with cannabis-infused dishes that reflect the state's agricultural heritage. From infused farm-to-table dinners to cannabis-infused beverages, Michigan's culinary cannabis scene is growing rapidly, offering consumers new and exciting ways to experience cannabis.

One of the most popular forms of cannabis-infused cuisine in Michigan is the cannabis-infused dinner. These multi-course meals are often held at private venues or pop-up restaurants, where chefs collaborate with cannabis producers to create dishes that highlight local ingredients and cannabis flavors. Each dish is carefully infused with low doses of THC or CBD, allowing diners to enjoy the effects of cannabis without becoming overly intoxicated. These dinners often pair cannabis-infused dishes with local wines or craft beers, creating a full sensory experience that celebrates both cannabis and Michigan's food culture.

In addition to infused dinners, Michigan is home to several cannabis bakeries and cafes that offer a variety of edibles, from brownies and cookies to infused coffees and teas. These establishments provide a casual setting where customers can enjoy cannabis-infused treats while socializing or working. Many of these bakeries and cafes also feature CBD-infused products, catering to consumers who are interested in the wellness benefits of cannabis without the psychoactive effects.

Cannabis-infused beverages are also becoming more popular in Michigan, with local producers creating everything from THC-infused sodas and tonics to CBD-infused sparkling waters. These beverages provide a convenient and discreet way to consume cannabis, offering an alternative to smoking or vaping. Many of these beverages are produced by small, independent companies that prioritize sustainability and local sourcing, reflecting Michigan's commitment to both quality and environmental responsibility.

Cannabis Tourism in Michigan

Cannabis tourism is a growing industry in Michigan, attracting visitors from across the country who are interested in exploring the state's cannabis culture. From cannabis-friendly hotels to guided dispensary tours, Michigan offers a variety of experiences for cannabis tourists.

One of the most popular attractions for cannabis tourists is the cannabis farm tour, which takes visitors behind the scenes of Michigan's cannabis cultivation industry. These tours often include visits to local grow facilities, where tourists can learn about the cultivation process, meet the growers, and sample fresh cannabis products. Some tours also offer workshops on sustainable growing practices and cannabis extraction techniques, providing a comprehensive look at Michigan's cannabis industry.

For those looking to combine cannabis with outdoor activities, Michigan offers cannabis-friendly retreats that cater to wellness and relaxation. These retreats often take place in scenic locations, such as the shores of Lake Michigan or the forests of Northern Michigan, and feature activities like yoga, hiking, and meditation. Participants can enjoy cannabis in a serene and natural setting, allowing them to connect with both the plant and their surroundings.

In cities like Detroit and Ann Arbor, cannabis tours take visitors on a guided journey through the state's best dispensaries, consumption lounges, and cannabis-related attractions. These tours provide an insider's look at Michigan's cannabis culture, with stops at iconic landmarks and opportunities to sample products from top producers.

Challenges and Opportunities in Michigan's Cannabis Market

While Michigan's cannabis industry has experienced significant growth, it has also faced challenges, particularly in terms of regulatory compliance and competition. The state's cannabis regulations are complex, with strict licensing requirements and compliance standards that can be difficult for small businesses to navigate. Additionally, Michigan's cannabis market is highly competitive, with a large number of dispensaries and growers vying for market share.

Despite these challenges, Michigan's cannabis industry continues to thrive, with opportunities for growth in areas such as cannabis tourism, craft cannabis, and sustainable cultivation. As the state continues to innovate, Michigan is well-positioned to become a leader in the national cannabis market, offering a unique blend of quality, community, and creativity.

Chapter 7: Massachusetts - Leading the East Coast Cannabis Revolution

Massachusetts has become a trailblazer in the cannabis industry, leading the charge on the East Coast with its progressive policies and commitment to social equity. Since the legalization of recreational cannabis in 2016 through the passage of Question 4, Massachusetts has transformed into a key player in the cannabis movement. The state's focus on responsible regulation, community involvement, and economic opportunity has set it apart as a model for cannabis legalization in other parts of the country.

Boston, the state's capital, serves as a hub for the cannabis industry, while smaller cities like Worcester and Springfield have embraced cannabis culture in their own ways. The state's cannabis industry is diverse and fast-growing, with dispensaries, cannabis-friendly events, and educational workshops springing up across Massachusetts. The state's progressive values, combined with its rich history of activism and innovation, have helped foster a unique and thriving cannabis culture.

The Dispensary Experience in Massachusetts

Massachusetts' dispensary scene reflects the state's commitment to responsible cannabis consumption and social equity. The state's regulations emphasize safety, education, and accessibility, ensuring that dispensaries offer a welcoming environment for both novice and experienced cannabis consumers. Many dispensaries in Massachusetts are designed with an upscale, boutique-style atmosphere, offering a personalized shopping experience that includes educational resources, knowledgeable staff, and a curated selection of products.

In cities like Boston, Cambridge, and Somerville, dispensaries are often integrated into the fabric of the community, with many shops focusing on local partnerships and community outreach. These dispensaries offer a wide range of products, including flower, concentrates, edibles, tinctures, and topicals. The state's rigorous testing and labeling requirements ensure that all products sold in dispensaries meet strict safety and quality standards, providing consumers with peace of mind.

One of the most notable aspects of Massachusetts' cannabis industry is its focus on social equity. The state has implemented a series of initiatives designed to help individuals from communities disproportionately impacted by the war on drugs enter the cannabis industry. These initiatives include reduced licensing fees, access to technical assistance, and priority status for social equity applicants. Many dispensaries in the state are owned and operated by individuals who have benefited from these programs, creating a diverse and inclusive cannabis industry.

Beyond the major cities, smaller towns across Massachusetts have also embraced cannabis culture, with dispensaries serving as gathering places for the local community. These shops often focus on supporting local growers and producers, offering craft cannabis strains that reflect the unique terroir of the region. Dispensaries in places like Northampton and Amherst have become hubs for cannabis education and activism, hosting workshops, community events, and advocacy efforts aimed at promoting responsible cannabis use.

Cannabis Festivals and Events in Massachusetts

Massachusetts is home to a number of cannabis festivals and events that celebrate the state's vibrant cannabis culture. These events provide a platform for cannabis enthusiasts, industry professionals, and advocates to come together and share their passion for the plant.

One of the most well-known events in the state is the Boston Freedom Rally, also known as Hempfest. Held annually on Boston Common, the Freedom Rally is a celebration of cannabis culture and advocacy, drawing thousands of attendees each year. The event features live music, speeches from cannabis advocates, vendor booths, and educational workshops on topics ranging from cannabis law to wellness applications. The Freedom Rally is more than just a festival—it is a symbol of Massachusetts' long-standing commitment to cannabis reform and social justice.

Another major event is the New England Cannabis Convention (NECANN), which takes place annually in Boston and brings together cannabis businesses, entrepreneurs, and consumers for a weekend of networking, product showcases, and educational panels. NECANN is one of the largest cannabis conventions on the East Coast, attracting industry professionals from across the region. The event offers valuable insights into the latest trends and innovations in the cannabis industry, making it a must-attend for anyone involved in the cannabis market.

In addition to these larger events, Massachusetts hosts a variety of smaller cannabis gatherings, including pop-up markets, infused yoga classes, and wellness retreats. These events often focus on specific aspects of cannabis culture, such as cannabis-infused cooking or CBD-based wellness practices, providing attendees with an opportunity to explore the many ways cannabis can enhance their lives.

Cannabis and Massachusetts' Food Culture

Massachusetts has a rich and diverse food culture, and cannabis has become an increasingly important part of the state's culinary scene. From cannabis-infused dinners to artisanal edibles, Massachusetts is leading the charge in exploring the intersection of cannabis and cuisine.

One of the most popular forms of cannabis-infused dining in Massachusetts is the infused dinner experience. These multi-course meals, often held at private venues or pop-up restaurants, feature dishes infused with THC or CBD, allowing diners to enjoy the effects of cannabis while savoring locally sourced ingredients. The meals are designed to provide a subtle cannabis experience, with low doses of THC that enhance the flavors of the food without overwhelming the diner. Many of these dinners also feature cannabis-infused beverages, such as THC-infused wines or cocktails, providing a complete sensory experience.

In addition to infused dinners, Massachusetts is home to several cannabis-friendly bakeries and cafes that offer a variety of edibles, from chocolates and gummies to CBD-infused coffees and teas. These establishments provide a casual setting where customers can enjoy cannabis-infused treats while socializing or working. Many of these bakeries and cafes also focus on using organic, locally sourced ingredients, reflecting Massachusetts' commitment to sustainability and quality.

Cannabis-infused beverages are also gaining popularity in Massachusetts, with local producers creating a range of THC and CBD-infused drinks. These beverages provide a convenient and discreet way to consume cannabis, offering an alternative to smoking or vaping. Many of these drinks are crafted with fresh, locally sourced ingredients and are designed to offer a refreshing, low-dose cannabis experience that is perfect for social settings.

Cannabis Tourism in Massachusetts

Cannabis tourism is a growing industry in Massachusetts, attracting visitors from across the country who are interested in exploring the state's cannabis culture. From cannabis-friendly hotels to guided dispensary tours, Massachusetts offers a variety of experiences for cannabis tourists.

One of the most popular attractions for cannabis tourists is the cannabis tour. These guided tours take visitors on a journey through Massachusetts' best dispensaries, grow facilities, and cannabis-related attractions. Tourists can learn about the cultivation and production process, meet local growers, and sample some of the state's finest cannabis products. Many tours also offer stops at iconic landmarks and opportunities to explore the state's rich history and culture.

For those looking to combine cannabis with wellness and relaxation, Massachusetts offers cannabis-friendly retreats that cater to health-conscious tourists. These retreats often take place in scenic locations, such as the Berkshires or Cape Cod, and feature activities like yoga, meditation, and hiking. Participants can enjoy cannabis in a serene and natural setting, allowing them to connect with both the plant and their surroundings.

In addition to wellness retreats, Massachusetts is home to several cannabis-friendly hotels and bed-and-breakfasts that cater to cannabis consumers. These accommodations offer designated smoking areas, cannabis-infused spa treatments, and curated cannabis experiences that allow guests to explore the state's cannabis scene in comfort and style.

Challenges and Opportunities in Massachusetts' Cannabis Market

While Massachusetts has enjoyed significant success as a leader in cannabis legalization, the state's cannabis industry has faced several challenges, particularly in terms of regulatory compliance and taxation. The state's strict regulations around cannabis advertising, packaging, and testing have made it difficult for some businesses to operate, particularly smaller companies that may not have the resources to meet these requirements.

High taxes on cannabis products have also been a point of contention, with some consumers opting to purchase from the black market to avoid paying the premium prices associated with legal cannabis. Despite these challenges, Massachusetts' cannabis industry continues to thrive, with dispensaries, events, and cannabis-related businesses attracting both locals and tourists.

One of the most exciting opportunities for growth in Massachusetts' cannabis market is the development of cannabis consumption lounges. These lounges are expected to become a major draw for both locals and tourists, offering a safe and legal space for cannabis consumption that aligns with the state's progressive values. As regulations around these lounges are finalized, many in the industry believe they will help solidify Massachusetts' status as a leader in the national cannabis market.

Massachusetts' cannabis industry also has the potential to lead in the area of sustainability, with many businesses focusing on eco-friendly cultivation practices, packaging solutions, and energy-efficient production methods. As consumers continue to demand high-quality, sustainably produced cannabis, Massachusetts is well-positioned to meet this growing demand and set a new standard for the industry.

Chapter 8: Illinois - Social Equity and the Future of Cannabis in the Midwest

Illinois stands out as a leader in the cannabis industry for its commitment to social equity and progressive policies. In 2019, Illinois became the first state to legalize recreational cannabis through legislative action rather than a voter initiative. The passage of the Cannabis Regulation and Tax Act was a landmark victory not only for cannabis reform but also for social justice, as the law included comprehensive provisions to address the harm caused by decades of cannabis prohibition, particularly in communities of color.

The state's cannabis culture is rapidly evolving, with a strong focus on diversity, equity, and inclusion. Chicago, the largest city in Illinois, has become a hub for the state's cannabis industry, with a thriving dispensary scene, cannabis-themed events, and a growing network of businesses dedicated to promoting social equity in the market. Illinois has also positioned itself as a leader in cannabis entrepreneurship, with initiatives aimed at supporting minority-owned businesses and individuals from communities disproportionately impacted by the war on drugs.

Illinois' Commitment to Social Equity

One of the most notable aspects of Illinois' cannabis legalization is its focus on social equity. The state's cannabis law includes provisions that prioritize licenses for individuals from communities disproportionately affected by cannabis prohibition. These social equity applicants are eligible for reduced licensing fees, access to low-interest loans, and technical assistance to help them establish and operate cannabis businesses.

Illinois also created a Cannabis Business Development Fund, which provides financial resources to social equity applicants, ensuring that individuals from historically marginalized communities have the opportunity to participate in the legal cannabis market. This fund is financed through a portion of the tax revenue generated by cannabis sales, creating a sustainable source of funding for social equity programs.

Additionally, Illinois' cannabis law includes a record expungement provision, which allows individuals with prior cannabis convictions to have their records cleared. This expungement process is one of the largest of its kind in the United States and is seen as a critical step in addressing the harm caused by cannabis prohibition. By offering individuals a clean slate, Illinois is helping to remove the barriers to employment and housing that often result from a criminal record, creating more opportunities for those impacted by the war on drugs to rebuild their lives.

The state's focus on social equity has made Illinois a model for other states looking to legalize cannabis in a way that prioritizes justice and inclusion. While the implementation of these programs has not been without its challenges, Illinois' commitment to creating an equitable cannabis industry has set a new standard for cannabis reform nationwide.

The Dispensary Scene in Illinois

Illinois' dispensary scene is as diverse as the state's population, with shops ranging from sleek, high-end retail spaces in Chicago to smaller, community-focused dispensaries in cities like Peoria and Champaign. The state's cannabis regulations require strict adherence to licensing, security, and quality control, ensuring that all products sold in dispensaries are safe, tested, and of the highest quality.

Chicago, in particular, has become a hub for cannabis businesses, with dispensaries offering a wide range of products, including flower, concentrates, edibles, tinctures, and topicals. Many dispensaries in the city prioritize social equity partnerships, working with local growers and businesses that reflect the state's commitment to diversity and inclusion. These partnerships often extend beyond the retail experience, with dispensaries hosting community events, educational workshops, and advocacy efforts aimed at promoting responsible cannabis use and supporting social equity initiatives.

Some of the most notable dispensaries in Chicago include Mindy's Edibles Dispensary, known for its artisanal edibles and upscale shopping experience, and Nature's Care Company, which focuses on wellness and natural healing through cannabis. These dispensaries offer a curated selection of products, with an emphasis on education and customer service. Many also offer delivery services and online ordering, making it easy for consumers to access their products.

Outside of Chicago, dispensaries in cities like Springfield, Rockford, and Evanston provide a more relaxed, community-oriented shopping experience. These dispensaries often focus on supporting local growers and offering products that reflect the unique character of the region. Whether in a bustling urban center or a quiet small town, Illinois' dispensaries offer something for every type of cannabis consumer.

Cannabis Festivals and Events in Illinois

Cannabis festivals and events have become a key part of Illinois' cannabis culture, providing a space for enthusiasts, industry professionals, and advocates to come together and celebrate the plant. These events often feature live music, educational workshops, vendor booths, and opportunities for networking and community building.

One of the most well-known events in Illinois is the Chicago Cannabis Expo, which brings together cannabis businesses, entrepreneurs, and consumers for a weekend of networking, product showcases, and educational panels. The expo is one of the largest cannabis conventions in the Midwest, attracting industry professionals from across the region. Attendees can explore the latest trends in cannabis, from cultivation techniques to new product innovations, and learn more about the state's social equity programs and business opportunities.

Another major event is the Illinois Cannabis Cup, a cannabis competition and festival that celebrates the best in the state's cannabis industry. The Cannabis Cup features live performances, product tastings, and awards ceremonies that recognize top growers, dispensaries, and cannabis brands. The event also includes educational panels on topics such as cannabis law, cultivation, and social equity, providing valuable insights for both consumers and industry professionals.

In addition to these larger events, Illinois hosts a variety of cannabis-friendly pop-up markets, infused yoga classes, and wellness retreats. These events often focus on specific aspects of cannabis culture, such as cannabis-infused cooking or CBD-based wellness practices, providing attendees with an opportunity to explore the many ways cannabis can enhance their lives.

Cannabis and Illinois' Food Culture

Illinois has a rich and diverse food scene, and cannabis has become an increasingly important part of the state's culinary landscape. From cannabis-infused dinners to artisanal edibles, Illinois is exploring the intersection of cannabis and cuisine in exciting and innovative ways.

One of the most popular forms of cannabis-infused dining in Illinois is the cannabis-infused dinner experience. These multi-course meals, often held at private venues or pop-up restaurants, feature dishes infused with THC or CBD, allowing diners to enjoy the effects of cannabis while savoring locally sourced ingredients. The meals are designed to provide a subtle cannabis experience, with low doses of THC that enhance the flavors of the food without overwhelming the diner. Many of these dinners also feature cannabis-infused beverages, such as THC-infused wines or cocktails, providing a complete sensory experience.

In addition to infused dinners, Illinois is home to several cannabis-friendly bakeries and cafes that offer a variety of edibles, from chocolates and gummies to CBD-infused coffees and teas. These establishments provide a casual setting where customers can enjoy cannabis-infused treats while socializing or working. Many of these bakeries and cafes also focus on using organic, locally sourced ingredients, reflecting Illinois' commitment to sustainability and quality.

Cannabis-infused beverages are also gaining popularity in Illinois, with local producers creating a range of THC and CBD-infused drinks. These beverages provide a convenient and discreet way to consume cannabis, offering an alternative to smoking or vaping. Many of these drinks are crafted with fresh, locally sourced ingredients and are designed to offer a refreshing, low-dose cannabis experience that is perfect for social settings.

Cannabis Tourism in Illinois

Cannabis tourism is a growing industry in Illinois, attracting visitors from across the country who are interested in exploring the state's cannabis culture. From cannabis-friendly hotels to guided dispensary tours, Illinois offers a variety of experiences for cannabis tourists.

One of the most popular attractions for cannabis tourists is the cannabis tour. These guided tours take visitors on a journey through Illinois' best dispensaries, grow facilities, and cannabis-related attractions. Tourists can learn about the cultivation and production process, meet local growers, and sample some of the state's finest cannabis products. Many tours also offer stops at iconic landmarks and opportunities to explore the state's rich history and culture.

For those looking to combine cannabis with wellness and relaxation, Illinois offers cannabis-friendly retreats that cater to health-conscious tourists. These retreats often take place in scenic locations, such as the Illinois River Valley or along Lake Michigan, and feature activities like yoga, meditation, and hiking. Participants can enjoy cannabis in a serene and natural setting, allowing them to connect with both the plant and their surroundings.

In addition to wellness retreats, Illinois is home to several cannabis-friendly hotels that cater to cannabis consumers. These accommodations offer designated smoking areas, cannabis-infused spa treatments, and curated cannabis experiences that allow guests to explore the state's cannabis scene in comfort and style.

Challenges and Opportunities in Illinois' Cannabis Market

Illinois has experienced significant success in its cannabis market, but the industry faces challenges, particularly in terms of regulatory compliance and taxation. The state's strict licensing and testing requirements have made it difficult for some businesses to enter the market, particularly smaller companies that may not have the resources to meet these requirements.

High taxes on cannabis products have also been a point of contention, with some consumers opting to purchase from the black market to avoid paying the premium prices associated with legal cannabis. Despite these challenges, Illinois' cannabis industry continues to grow, with new dispensaries and cannabis-related businesses opening regularly.

One of the most exciting opportunities for growth in Illinois' cannabis market is the development of social equity programs. These programs are designed to ensure that individuals from communities disproportionately impacted by cannabis prohibition have the opportunity to participate in the legal cannabis market. As Illinois continues to refine its social equity initiatives, the state has the potential to set a new standard for cannabis reform, creating a more inclusive and just industry.

Chapter 9: Florida - The Road to Full Legalization

Florida stands at a pivotal moment in its cannabis journey, with a thriving medical cannabis market and a growing movement for full recreational legalization. Although recreational cannabis is not yet legal in the state, Florida's medical cannabis program has become one of the largest in the United States, with hundreds of thousands of registered patients and a booming network of dispensaries. The state's unique demographics—ranging from a large retiree population to a vibrant tourism industry—have created a distinctive cannabis culture that continues to evolve.

Florida's cannabis market is marked by its focus on wellness, medical use, and a burgeoning interest in recreational legalization. The state's warm climate and diverse population make it an ideal location for both cannabis cultivation and consumption. With cities like Miami, Orlando, and Tampa embracing cannabis culture, and cannabis tourism on the rise, Florida is positioning itself as a major player in the national cannabis industry.

Medical Cannabis in Florida: A Booming Market

Florida's journey toward cannabis reform began with the legalization of medical cannabis in 2016 through the passage of Amendment 2, which allowed patients with qualifying medical conditions to access cannabis under the supervision of a physician. The state's medical cannabis program has since grown exponentially, serving patients with conditions such as chronic pain, cancer, epilepsy, PTSD, and more.

Florida's medical cannabis dispensaries are widespread, with many offering a variety of products, including flower, edibles, tinctures, and topicals. The state's dispensary scene reflects its focus on wellness and medical use, with many shops offering products tailored to the needs of patients seeking relief from specific conditions. Dispensaries in cities like Miami, Orlando, and Tampa cater to a diverse range of consumers, from elderly patients to younger adults interested in wellness-focused cannabis products.

One of the unique aspects of Florida's medical cannabis market is the emphasis on CBD-rich products. Given the state's large retiree population, many patients prefer non-psychoactive CBD products for pain management, anxiety relief, and overall wellness. Dispensaries in Florida often feature a wide selection of CBD products, including oils, capsules, and topicals, making cannabis accessible to patients who may be new to cannabis or hesitant about the effects of THC.

Cannabis Culture in Florida's Major Cities

Florida's cannabis culture is most evident in its major cities, where dispensaries, events, and cannabis-friendly businesses have begun to flourish. Miami, in particular, has emerged as a hub for cannabis culture, with the city's vibrant nightlife and diverse population embracing cannabis as part of the broader wellness and lifestyle scene.

In Miami, cannabis is often integrated into the city's art and music festivals, with events like Art Basel Miami featuring cannabis-friendly installations and pop-up dispensaries. The city's unique blend of Latin American and Caribbean influences has also shaped its cannabis culture, with many local businesses offering infused foods and beverages that reflect Miami's culinary diversity. From CBD-infused mojitos to cannabis-infused tropical treats, Miami's food scene is quickly becoming a destination for cannabis enthusiasts.

Orlando and Tampa are also embracing cannabis culture, with dispensaries and cannabis-related businesses popping up throughout the cities. Orlando, home to many of the state's top tourist attractions, has seen a rise in cannabis tourism, with visitors seeking out cannabis-friendly experiences while exploring the city's theme parks and entertainment districts. Tampa, known for its vibrant cultural scene, has become a hub for cannabis wellness retreats, where participants can enjoy yoga, meditation, and cannabis-infused spa treatments.

Cannabis Tourism in Florida

Florida's tourism industry is one of the largest in the country, and cannabis is beginning to play a role in the state's appeal to visitors. While recreational cannabis remains illegal, cannabis tourism is growing, particularly in cities like Miami and Orlando, where tourists can explore the state's medical cannabis dispensaries and cannabis-friendly accommodations.

One of the most popular attractions for cannabis tourists is the cannabis farm tour, which takes visitors behind the scenes of Florida's cannabis cultivation industry. These tours often include visits to local grow facilities, where tourists can learn about the cultivation process, meet the growers, and sample fresh cannabis products. Some tours also offer workshops on sustainable growing practices and cannabis extraction techniques, providing a comprehensive look at Florida's cannabis industry.

In addition to farm tours, Florida is home to several cannabis-friendly hotels and bed-and-breakfasts that cater to cannabis consumers. These accommodations offer designated smoking areas, cannabis-infused spa treatments, and curated cannabis experiences that allow guests to explore the state's cannabis scene in comfort and style. For those looking to combine cannabis with wellness and relaxation, Florida offers cannabis-friendly retreats that cater to health-conscious tourists. These retreats often take place in scenic locations, such as the Florida Keys or along the Gulf Coast, and feature activities like yoga, meditation, and hiking.

Cannabis and Florida's Food Culture

Florida's culinary scene has always been a major draw for tourists and locals alike, and cannabis-infused cuisine is becoming an increasingly important part of that landscape. The state's diverse population, which includes significant Latin American and Caribbean communities, has influenced the way cannabis is incorporated into food, with chefs experimenting with cannabis-infused dishes that reflect Florida's rich culinary heritage.

One of the most popular forms of cannabis-infused dining in Florida is the infused dinner experience. These multi-course meals are often held at private venues or pop-up restaurants, where chefs collaborate with cannabis producers to create dishes that highlight local ingredients and cannabis flavors. Each dish is carefully infused with low doses of THC or CBD, allowing diners to enjoy the effects of cannabis without becoming overly intoxicated. These dinners often pair cannabis-infused dishes with Florida-inspired cocktails or mocktails, creating a full sensory experience that celebrates both cannabis and Florida's culinary culture.

In addition to infused dinners, Florida is home to several cannabis-friendly cafes and bakeries that offer a variety of edibles, from tropical-infused gummies to CBD-infused coffees. These establishments provide a casual setting where customers can enjoy cannabis-infused treats while socializing or working. Many of these cafes also feature CBD-infused smoothies, teas, and juices, catering to consumers who are interested in the wellness benefits of cannabis.

The Path to Recreational Legalization in Florida

While medical cannabis is thriving in Florida, the state has yet to legalize recreational cannabis. Efforts to legalize recreational cannabis through the state legislature have faced significant opposition, particularly from conservative lawmakers and interest groups. However, advocates for legalization are pushing for a voter initiative in the near future, similar to the one that legalized medical cannabis.

Public opinion polls show that a majority of Floridians support the legalization of recreational cannabis, suggesting that it may only be a matter of time before the state takes the next step toward full legalization. The potential for recreational cannabis in Florida is vast, particularly given the state's large tourism industry and diverse population. Many believe that Florida's cannabis market could rival that of California or Colorado if recreational legalization is achieved.

Challenges and Opportunities in Florida's Cannabis Industry

Florida's cannabis industry faces several challenges, particularly in terms of regulation and accessibility. The state's medical cannabis program is heavily regulated, with strict licensing requirements and limitations on the number of dispensaries allowed to operate. Additionally, Florida's cannabis laws prohibit smokable flower, which has limited the range of products available to patients. However, a recent court ruling overturned this ban, allowing smokable cannabis to be sold in dispensaries for the first time.

Another challenge is the cost of entry into the cannabis market. The state's licensing fees and regulatory compliance costs are among the highest in the country, making it difficult for small businesses to compete. This has led to concerns about the monopolization of the market by a few large companies, which control the majority of dispensaries and grow facilities in the state.

Despite these challenges, Florida's cannabis industry continues to grow, with opportunities for expansion in areas such as cannabis tourism, cannabis-infused cuisine, and wellness retreats. As the state moves toward potential recreational legalization, Florida has the opportunity to become a leader in the national cannabis market, offering unique experiences that reflect the state's diverse culture and appeal to tourists from around the world.

Chapter 10: New York - Cannabis in the Cultural Capital of the World

New York has long been a cultural epicenter, influencing trends in fashion, music, art, and now cannabis. With the legalization of recreational cannabis in 2021, New York became the largest state on the East Coast to embrace cannabis reform, setting the stage for a dynamic and thriving cannabis industry. The state's commitment to social equity, public health, and economic opportunity has positioned it as a leader in the national cannabis movement.

New York City, in particular, is set to become a major hub for the cannabis industry, with its diverse population, vibrant nightlife, and rich cultural history creating a unique environment for the development of a cannabis culture unlike any other. From cannabis-infused dining experiences to social consumption lounges, New York's cannabis scene is poised to shape the future of the industry in ways that reflect the city's creativity and innovation.

New York's Path to Legalization

New York's journey to cannabis legalization was a long and complex process, marked by years of advocacy, activism, and political debate. The state's medical cannabis program, which began in 2014, provided a foundation for the eventual legalization of recreational cannabis. However, it wasn't until March 2021, with the passage of the Marijuana Regulation and Taxation Act (MRTA), that adult-use cannabis became legal in New York.

One of the key elements of the MRTA is its focus on social equity. The law includes provisions to address the disproportionate impact of cannabis prohibition on communities of color, with 40% of tax revenue from cannabis sales earmarked for reinvestment in these communities. The law also includes a comprehensive expungement program, allowing individuals with prior cannabis convictions to have their records cleared.

New York's cannabis legalization is seen as a major victory for both cannabis advocates and social justice reformers, with the state's approach to legalization serving as a model for other states looking to prioritize equity in their cannabis markets.

The Dispensary Experience in New York

While the first legal adult-use dispensaries in New York are not expected to open until 2023, the state's existing medical dispensaries have already set a high standard for the retail experience. Dispensaries in New York City and other major metropolitan areas are designed to offer a luxurious and educational environment, with knowledgeable staff on hand to guide customers through their product selections.

Many dispensaries focus on providing a wellness-oriented experience, offering products tailored to medical patients and health-conscious consumers. The state's strict regulations around product testing and labeling ensure that all products sold in dispensaries meet the highest standards of safety and quality. In addition to flower, New York's dispensaries offer a wide variety of products, including edibles, tinctures, topicals, and vape cartridges.

One of the most anticipated developments in New York's cannabis market is the opening of social consumption lounges, which will provide a legal and safe space for adults to consume cannabis in a social setting. These lounges are expected to become a major draw for both locals and tourists, offering a new kind of nightlife experience that reflects New York's reputation as a global cultural hub.

Cannabis and New York's Cultural Scene

New York City is known for its rich cultural scene, and cannabis is quickly becoming a part of that landscape. From cannabis-infused dining experiences to cannabis-themed art shows, the city's creative community is embracing cannabis as both an inspiration and an integral part of the artistic process.

Cannabis-infused dinners have become particularly popular in New York, with chefs collaborating with cannabis producers to create multi-course meals that highlight local ingredients and cannabis flavors. These dinners are often paired with cannabis-infused cocktails or mocktails, providing a full sensory experience that blends cannabis with the city's renowned culinary scene. Many of these events are held at private venues or pop-up restaurants, offering an intimate and exclusive dining experience.

In addition to cannabis-infused cuisine, cannabis-themed art shows and live performances are becoming more common throughout the city. These events often feature local artists who explore the relationship between cannabis and creativity through various mediums, including painting, sculpture, and performance art. Cannabis-friendly venues are also starting to host live music and comedy shows, where patrons can enjoy cannabis in a relaxed and social setting.

Cannabis Festivals and Events in New York

New York is home to a number of cannabis festivals and events that celebrate the state's emerging cannabis culture. These events provide a platform for cannabis enthusiasts, industry professionals, and advocates to come together and share their passion for the plant.

One of the most anticipated events is the New York Cannabis Expo, which will bring together cannabis businesses, entrepreneurs, and consumers for a weekend of networking, product showcases, and educational panels. The expo will provide valuable insights into the latest trends and innovations in the cannabis industry, making it a must-attend event for anyone involved in the market.

Another major event is the New York City Cannabis Parade and Rally, which has been held annually since 1973 and is one of the longest-running cannabis advocacy events in the world. The parade and rally bring together cannabis activists, community leaders, and supporters to march through the streets of Manhattan in support of cannabis reform. The event features speeches from cannabis advocates, live music, and vendor booths, making it a celebration of cannabis culture and activism.

In addition to these larger events, New York is home to a variety of cannabis-friendly pop-up markets, yoga classes, and wellness retreats. These events often focus on specific aspects of cannabis culture, such as cannabis-infused cooking or CBD-based wellness practices, providing attendees with an opportunity to explore the many ways cannabis can enhance their lives.

Cannabis Tourism in New York

New York is already one of the most popular tourist destinations in the world, and cannabis is expected to become an integral part of the city's tourism industry. From cannabis-friendly hotels to guided dispensary tours, New York offers a variety of experiences for cannabis tourists.

One of the most popular attractions for cannabis tourists is the cannabis tour, which takes visitors on a journey through New York's best dispensaries, grow facilities, and cannabis-related attractions. Tourists can learn about the cultivation and production process, meet local growers, and sample some of the state's finest cannabis products. Many tours also offer stops at iconic landmarks, such as the Empire State Building and Central Park, allowing visitors to explore the city's rich history and culture while enjoying cannabis.

For those looking to combine cannabis with wellness and relaxation, New York offers cannabis-friendly retreats that cater to health-conscious tourists. These retreats often take place in scenic locations, such as the Catskills or the Hudson Valley, and feature activities like yoga, meditation, and hiking. Participants can enjoy cannabis in a serene and natural setting, allowing them to connect with both the plant and their surroundings.

In addition to wellness retreats, New York is home to several cannabis-friendly hotels and luxury accommodations that cater to cannabis consumers. These establishments offer designated smoking areas, cannabis-infused spa treatments, and curated cannabis experiences that allow guests to explore the state's cannabis scene in comfort and style.

Challenges and Opportunities in New York's Cannabis Market

While New York's cannabis industry holds significant promise, it also faces challenges, particularly in terms of regulation and accessibility. The state's cannabis regulations are among the most comprehensive in the country, with strict requirements for licensing, testing, and social equity. While these regulations are intended to ensure consumer safety and promote equity, they have also created barriers to entry for some small businesses and entrepreneurs.

Another challenge is the high cost of doing business in New York, particularly in cities like New York City, where rent and operational costs can be prohibitively expensive. This has led to concerns about the monopolization of the market by large, well-funded companies, which may have an advantage over smaller, locally owned businesses.

Despite these challenges, New York's cannabis industry offers significant opportunities for growth, particularly in areas such as social consumption lounges, cannabis tourism, and cannabis-infused dining. As the state continues to develop its regulatory framework and expand its social equity programs, New York is poised to become a global leader in the cannabis industry, offering a unique and diverse cannabis culture that reflects the city's status as a cultural capital.

Chapter 11: New Jersey - Cannabis on the Rise in the Garden State

New Jersey has emerged as a significant player in the cannabis industry following the legalization of recreational cannabis in 2020. As one of the first East Coast states to fully legalize adult-use cannabis, New Jersey has quickly positioned itself as a key market in the rapidly expanding national cannabis landscape. With its proximity to major metropolitan areas like New York City and Philadelphia, New Jersey is poised to become a hub for cannabis businesses and tourism in the region.

The state's cannabis culture is still in its early stages but is evolving rapidly as dispensaries open, events take shape, and cannabis becomes integrated into the social fabric of New Jersey's cities and towns. From urban centers like Newark and Jersey City to smaller towns along the coast, cannabis is beginning to have a noticeable impact on New Jersey's economy, culture, and community.

The Path to Legalization in New Jersey

New Jersey's journey to cannabis legalization was largely driven by a combination of public advocacy and political momentum. After several years of debate, New Jersey voters overwhelmingly approved Question 1, a ballot measure to legalize recreational cannabis, in the November 2020 election. The result reflected a growing shift in public opinion in favor of cannabis reform, driven by concerns over racial justice, economic opportunity, and public health.

Following the vote, the state passed the New Jersey Cannabis Regulatory, Enforcement Assistance, and Marketplace Modernization Act, which created the legal framework for the regulation and sale of adult-use cannabis. The law included strong provisions for social equity, ensuring that communities disproportionately impacted by cannabis prohibition would have access to the legal market.

New Jersey's legalization law has been hailed as one of the most progressive in the country, particularly in its emphasis on expungement and social equity licensing. The state's expungement program allows individuals with prior cannabis convictions to have their records cleared, removing barriers to employment, housing, and other opportunities. In addition, the state's social equity program prioritizes licenses for individuals from communities disproportionately harmed by the war on drugs, creating opportunities for minority-owned and small businesses to participate in the legal cannabis market.

The Dispensary Scene in New Jersey

New Jersey's dispensary scene is still in its early stages, but it is growing rapidly as more businesses receive licenses to operate in the state. The state's existing medical cannabis dispensaries have already begun to transition to serving both medical and recreational consumers, offering a variety of products, including flower, edibles, tinctures, and topicals.

In cities like Newark, Jersey City, and Trenton, dispensaries are emerging as key destinations for both locals and tourists looking to explore the state's legal cannabis market. These dispensaries are often designed with an upscale, boutique-style aesthetic, offering a welcoming and educational environment for customers. Knowledgeable budtenders are available to assist both novice and experienced consumers, providing guidance on product selection, dosage, and consumption methods.

Many of New Jersey's dispensaries also focus on social responsibility and community engagement, partnering with local organizations to support social equity initiatives and promote responsible cannabis use. Dispensaries in the state are required to adhere to strict regulations around product testing, labeling, and security, ensuring that all products sold are safe, tested, and of high quality.

As the market continues to grow, New Jersey is expected to see the rise of cannabis consumption lounges, which will provide legal and safe spaces for adults to consume cannabis in a social setting. These lounges, which are expected to open in major cities and tourist areas, will offer a new kind of nightlife experience that reflects New Jersey's unique cannabis culture.

Cannabis and New Jersey's Cultural Scene

Cannabis is quickly becoming a part of New Jersey's cultural fabric, with the state's creative community embracing cannabis as both an inspiration and a central element of their work. From art exhibitions to live music events, cannabis is being integrated into New Jersey's thriving arts and entertainment scene.

Cannabis-infused dinners are becoming particularly popular in New Jersey, with chefs collaborating with cannabis producers to create gourmet meals that highlight local ingredients and cannabis flavors. These dinners are often held at private venues or pop-up restaurants, offering an intimate and exclusive dining experience that blends cannabis with New Jersey's renowned food culture. Many of these events also feature cannabis-infused cocktails or mocktails, providing a full sensory experience for attendees.

In addition to infused dining, cannabis-friendly art shows and live performances are becoming more common throughout the state. These events often feature local artists and performers who explore the relationship between cannabis and creativity through various mediums, including painting, sculpture, and performance art. Cannabis-friendly venues are also starting to host live music and comedy shows, where patrons can enjoy cannabis in a relaxed and social setting.

Cannabis Festivals and Events in New Jersey

As the cannabis industry continues to grow in New Jersey, so too does the number of cannabis-related festivals and events. These gatherings provide a platform for cannabis enthusiasts, industry professionals, and advocates to come together and celebrate the state's emerging cannabis culture.

One of the most anticipated events is the New Jersey Cannabis Expo, which will bring together cannabis businesses, entrepreneurs, and consumers for a weekend of networking, product showcases, and educational panels. The expo will provide valuable insights into the latest trends and innovations in the cannabis industry, making it a must-attend event for anyone involved in the market.

Another major event is the Garden State Cannabis Festival, a celebration of cannabis culture that features live music, food vendors, and educational workshops on topics such as cannabis law, cultivation, and social equity. The festival is expected to become one of the state's premier cannabis events, drawing attendees from across the region.

In addition to these larger events, New Jersey is home to a variety of cannabis-friendly pop-up markets, yoga classes, and wellness retreats. These events often focus on specific aspects of cannabis culture, such as cannabis-infused cooking or CBD-based wellness practices, providing attendees with an opportunity to explore the many ways cannabis can enhance their lives.

Cannabis Tourism in New Jersey

New Jersey's location in the heart of the Northeast corridor, with easy access to major cities like New York and Philadelphia, makes it an ideal destination for cannabis tourism. As more dispensaries open and consumption lounges become available, New Jersey is expected to attract visitors from across the region who are interested in exploring the state's cannabis culture.

One of the most popular attractions for cannabis tourists is the cannabis tour, which takes visitors on a journey through New Jersey's best dispensaries, grow facilities, and cannabis-related attractions. Tourists can learn about the cultivation and production process, meet local growers, and sample some of the state's finest cannabis products. Many tours also offer stops at iconic landmarks and opportunities to explore the state's rich history and culture.

For those looking to combine cannabis with wellness and relaxation, New Jersey offers cannabis-friendly retreats that cater to health-conscious tourists. These retreats often take place in scenic locations, such as the Jersey Shore or the Pine Barrens, and feature activities like yoga, meditation, and hiking. Participants can enjoy cannabis in a serene and natural setting, allowing them to connect with both the plant and their surroundings.

In addition to wellness retreats, New Jersey is home to several cannabis-friendly hotels and luxury accommodations that cater to cannabis consumers. These establishments offer designated smoking areas, cannabis-infused spa treatments, and curated cannabis experiences that allow guests to explore the state's cannabis scene in comfort and style.

Challenges and Opportunities in New Jersey's Cannabis Market

While New Jersey's cannabis market holds significant promise, it also faces challenges, particularly in terms of regulation and accessibility. The state's cannabis regulations are among the most comprehensive in the country, with strict requirements for licensing, testing, and social equity. While these regulations are intended to ensure consumer safety and promote equity, they have also created barriers to entry for some small businesses and entrepreneurs.

Another challenge is the high cost of doing business in New Jersey, particularly in cities like Newark and Jersey City, where rent and operational costs can be prohibitively expensive. This has led to concerns about the monopolization of the market by large, well-funded companies, which may have an advantage over smaller, locally owned businesses.

Despite these challenges, New Jersey's cannabis industry offers significant opportunities for growth, particularly in areas such as cannabis tourism, social consumption lounges, and cannabis-infused dining. As the state continues to develop its regulatory framework and expand its social equity programs, New Jersey is poised to become a leader in the East Coast cannabis market, offering a unique and diverse cannabis culture that reflects the state's rich history and vibrant communities.

Chapter 12: Pennsylvania - The Potential for Cannabis Growth in the Keystone State

Pennsylvania has long been seen as a critical state in shaping national political and economic trends, and its role in the cannabis movement is no different. Though Pennsylvania has yet to legalize recreational cannabis, its robust medical cannabis program has become one of the largest in the United States. The state's medical cannabis market is growing rapidly, with dispensaries, cultivators, and producers creating a strong foundation for what could become a major recreational cannabis market in the future.

The state's mix of urban centers like Philadelphia and Pittsburgh, combined with its rural and agricultural communities, has created a unique cannabis landscape. Pennsylvania's commitment to social justice and public health reform has driven its approach to cannabis policy, while the state's burgeoning cannabis culture is reflected in its festivals, wellness retreats, and cannabis-friendly businesses. As the push for recreational legalization intensifies, Pennsylvania stands at the crossroads of becoming a key player in the cannabis industry.

Medical Cannabis in Pennsylvania: A Growing Market

Pennsylvania's journey into the cannabis industry began with the legalization of medical cannabis in 2016, following the passage of Senate Bill 3, which created the state's medical cannabis program. The law allowed patients with qualifying medical conditions to access cannabis products under the supervision of a physician. Since then, the program has grown to serve over 500,000 registered patients, making it one of the largest medical cannabis markets in the country.

The state's medical cannabis dispensaries are widespread, with many offering a variety of products tailored to the needs of patients. From flower and concentrates to tinctures, edibles, and topicals, Pennsylvania's dispensaries cater to a diverse range of consumers seeking relief from conditions such as chronic pain, epilepsy, PTSD, and cancer. The state's dispensary scene reflects its focus on wellness, with many shops designed to offer a clean, professional, and welcoming environment for patients.

CBD-rich products are particularly popular in Pennsylvania, with many medical patients opting for non-psychoactive CBD products to manage pain, anxiety, and inflammation. The state's dispensaries offer a wide range of CBD products, including oils, capsules, and topicals, making cannabis accessible to patients who may be new to the plant or hesitant about the effects of THC.

The Push for Recreational Legalization

While Pennsylvania's medical cannabis market is thriving, the push for recreational legalization has gained significant momentum in recent years. Public opinion polls show that a majority of Pennsylvanians support the legalization of recreational cannabis, and many lawmakers are advocating for a more progressive approach to cannabis reform.

However, the path to legalization has been met with resistance from some political leaders, particularly in the state legislature. Despite this, advocates for cannabis reform continue to push for a legislative solution, with many believing that recreational legalization could be achieved through a voter initiative or future legislative action. If Pennsylvania were to legalize recreational cannabis, it would likely become one of the largest cannabis markets on the East Coast, given its population size and economic potential.

The economic benefits of legalization, including the potential for job creation, tax revenue, and business development, are key factors driving the conversation. Many experts believe that Pennsylvania's agricultural industry could play a significant role in the cannabis market, with the state's large rural areas offering ideal conditions for cannabis cultivation.

The Dispensary Scene in Pennsylvania

Pennsylvania's medical cannabis dispensaries offer a diverse range of products and services, with dispensaries in cities like Philadelphia, Pittsburgh, and Harrisburg leading the way. These dispensaries are often designed with a focus on education and wellness, providing patients with access to high-quality cannabis products and knowledgeable staff who can guide them through the process of selecting the right product for their needs.

In Philadelphia, the state's largest city, dispensaries cater to a wide range of medical patients, from seniors seeking relief from chronic pain to younger adults managing anxiety and PTSD. Philadelphia's dispensaries are often located in trendy neighborhoods, with shops offering a boutique-style shopping experience. Many dispensaries also host educational workshops and community events, creating a space where patients can learn more about cannabis and connect with others who are using it for wellness purposes.

Outside of the major cities, smaller towns and rural areas in Pennsylvania are also embracing cannabis culture, with dispensaries offering a more intimate, community-focused experience. These dispensaries often focus on supporting local growers and producers, offering products that are unique to the region. In many cases, the dispensary staff are also local, with a deep knowledge of the products they sell and a commitment to providing personalized care to their patients.

Cannabis Festivals and Events in Pennsylvania

Cannabis festivals and events are becoming a key part of Pennsylvania's cannabis culture, providing a platform for patients, advocates, and industry professionals to come together and celebrate the plant. These events often feature live music, educational workshops, vendor booths, and opportunities for networking and community building.

One of the most well-known cannabis events in Pennsylvania is the Philadelphia Cannabis Festival, an annual event that brings together cannabis enthusiasts, industry leaders, and advocates for a day of music, education, and celebration. The festival features keynote speakers, product demonstrations, and opportunities for attendees to learn more about the state's medical cannabis program and the push for recreational legalization.

Another major event is the Pittsburgh Medical Cannabis Expo, which focuses on the medical cannabis industry and provides valuable insights into the latest trends in cannabis wellness, research, and business development. The expo is a must-attend event for anyone involved in the medical cannabis industry, offering educational panels, product showcases, and opportunities for networking with industry professionals.

In addition to these larger events, Pennsylvania hosts a variety of cannabis-friendly pop-up markets, yoga classes, and wellness retreats. These events often focus on specific aspects of cannabis culture, such as cannabis-infused cooking or CBD-based wellness practices, providing attendees with an opportunity to explore the many ways cannabis can enhance their lives.

Cannabis and Pennsylvania's Food Culture

Pennsylvania's food scene has a rich history, with cities like Philadelphia known for their iconic dishes, including cheesesteaks, soft pretzels, and hoagies. Cannabis is beginning to make its mark on the state's culinary landscape, with chefs and producers experimenting with cannabis-infused dishes that reflect Pennsylvania's unique food culture.

Cannabis-infused dinners are becoming increasingly popular in Pennsylvania, with chefs collaborating with cannabis producers to create multi-course meals that highlight local ingredients and cannabis flavors. These dinners often feature dishes infused with low doses of THC or CBD, allowing diners to enjoy the effects of cannabis without becoming overly intoxicated. Many of these meals are held at private venues or pop-up restaurants, providing an intimate and exclusive dining experience.

In addition to infused dinners, Pennsylvania is home to several cannabis-friendly cafes and bakeries that offer a variety of edibles, from baked goods to infused coffees and teas. These establishments provide a casual setting where customers can enjoy cannabis-infused treats while socializing or working. Many cafes and bakeries in cities like Philadelphia and Pittsburgh are beginning to incorporate CBD-infused products into their menus, catering to consumers who are interested in the wellness benefits of cannabis.

Challenges and Opportunities in Pennsylvania's Cannabis Market

While Pennsylvania's medical cannabis industry has experienced significant growth, the state faces several challenges, particularly in terms of regulatory compliance and the push for recreational legalization. The state's medical cannabis program is heavily regulated, with strict licensing requirements and limitations on the number of dispensaries allowed to operate. This has created barriers to entry for some small businesses, leading to concerns about the monopolization of the market by a few large companies.

Another challenge is the high cost of medical cannabis in Pennsylvania. Patients often pay more for cannabis products in the state than they would in other markets, due to a combination of supply limitations, taxation, and regulatory costs. This has led to calls for reform within the medical cannabis program to make cannabis more affordable and accessible to patients.

Despite these challenges, Pennsylvania's cannabis industry continues to grow, with opportunities for expansion in areas such as cannabis tourism, agricultural cultivation, and social equity initiatives. As the state moves toward potential recreational legalization, Pennsylvania has the opportunity to become a leader in the national cannabis market, offering unique experiences that reflect the state's rich history and diverse culture.

Chapter 13: Arizona - The Southwest's Cannabis Frontier

Arizona's path to cannabis legalization is a story of persistence and progress, as the state has transformed from a traditionally conservative region to one of the leading cannabis markets in the Southwest. With the legalization of recreational cannabis in 2020 through Proposition 207, Arizona has established itself as a frontier for cannabis innovation and business development. The state's booming market is fueled by a combination of favorable business conditions, expansive desert landscapes, and a growing demand for cannabis products across both urban and rural areas.

Phoenix, the state's capital and largest city, has become a hub for cannabis culture and commerce, while cities like Tucson and Flagstaff have embraced cannabis as part of their local economies. Arizona's diverse landscape and vibrant tourism industry make it an ideal destination for cannabis enthusiasts seeking a mix of adventure, relaxation, and wellness.

Proposition 207: Legalizing Recreational Cannabis in Arizona

The passage of Proposition 207, also known as the Smart and Safe Arizona Act, was a major victory for cannabis advocates in the state. After years of debate and failed attempts to legalize recreational cannabis, Arizona voters approved the measure in November 2020, allowing adults over the age of 21 to possess, purchase, and consume cannabis legally. The law also included provisions for the expungement of certain cannabis-related offenses, helping to address the impact of cannabis prohibition on communities of color.

Proposition 207 created a regulatory framework for the sale of recreational cannabis, including strict guidelines around licensing, product testing, and security. The law also established a tax on cannabis sales, with a portion of the revenue allocated to public health programs, education, and infrastructure projects. This tax revenue has already generated millions of dollars for the state, providing a significant economic boost as Arizona continues to recover from the effects of the COVID-19 pandemic.

The legalization of recreational cannabis in Arizona has transformed the state's cannabis industry, with dispensaries, cultivators, and producers expanding rapidly to meet the growing demand. Arizona's cannabis market is now one of the largest in the Southwest, attracting businesses and consumers from across the region.

The Dispensary Scene in Arizona

Arizona's dispensary scene is thriving, with over 100 licensed dispensaries operating throughout the state. These dispensaries offer a wide range of products, from traditional flower and concentrates to edibles, tinctures, and topicals. Dispensaries in cities like Phoenix, Tucson, and Scottsdale cater to a diverse range of consumers, from medical patients seeking relief to recreational users looking for premium products.

Phoenix, in particular, has emerged as a major center for cannabis retail, with dispensaries offering a luxurious and modern shopping experience. Many of these dispensaries feature sleek, high-end interiors, knowledgeable staff, and a wide selection of products sourced from local cultivators. Phoenix's dispensaries often prioritize customer education, providing resources on cannabis consumption methods, dosage, and product selection.

In addition to traditional dispensaries, Arizona has embraced delivery services, allowing consumers to purchase cannabis products online and have them delivered directly to their homes. This has made cannabis more accessible, particularly in rural areas where dispensaries may be limited. As Arizona's cannabis market continues to grow, more dispensaries and delivery services are expected to open, offering consumers even greater access to high-quality cannabis products.

Cannabis Culture in Arizona's Major Cities

Cannabis culture in Arizona is rapidly evolving, with cities like Phoenix, Tucson, and Flagstaff leading the way in integrating cannabis into their local economies and social scenes. In Phoenix, cannabis is becoming a central part of the city's arts and entertainment culture, with cannabis-friendly events, festivals, and businesses springing up across the city.

Cannabis-infused dinners have become particularly popular in Arizona, with chefs collaborating with cannabis producers to create multi-course meals that highlight local ingredients and cannabis flavors. These dinners are often held at private venues or pop-up restaurants, providing an intimate and exclusive dining experience for cannabis enthusiasts. Many of these meals are paired with cannabis-infused beverages or mocktails, offering a full sensory experience that combines cannabis with Arizona's culinary traditions.

Tucson, known for its vibrant arts scene and desert landscapes, has also embraced cannabis culture, with dispensaries and wellness retreats becoming popular destinations for both locals and tourists. In Flagstaff, a college town located near the Grand Canyon, cannabis has become a part of the city's laid-back, outdoor lifestyle, with cannabis-friendly hiking tours and wellness experiences attracting visitors looking to enjoy cannabis in nature.

Cannabis Tourism in Arizona

Arizona's stunning desert landscapes and thriving tourism industry make it an ideal destination for cannabis tourism. With recreational cannabis now legal, visitors can explore the state's dispensaries, cannabis-friendly accommodations, and outdoor adventures while enjoying the unique beauty of the Southwest.

One of the most popular attractions for cannabis tourists is the cannabis hiking tour, which takes visitors on guided hikes through Arizona's iconic desert landscapes, including the Grand Canyon, Sedona, and Saguaro National Park. These tours often include stops at scenic overlooks, where tourists can enjoy cannabis in a natural setting while taking in the breathtaking views of Arizona's red rock formations and desert sunsets.

For those looking to combine cannabis with wellness and relaxation, Arizona offers cannabis-friendly retreats that cater to health-conscious tourists. These retreats often take place in luxury resorts or wellness centers, featuring activities like yoga, meditation, and spa treatments. Participants can enjoy cannabis in a serene and tranquil environment, allowing them to relax and rejuvenate while connecting with the natural beauty of Arizona's desert landscapes.

In addition to wellness retreats, Arizona is home to several cannabis-friendly hotels and bed-and-breakfasts that offer accommodations designed specifically for cannabis consumers. These establishments provide designated smoking areas, cannabis-infused spa treatments, and curated cannabis experiences that allow guests to explore the state's cannabis scene in comfort and style.

Cannabis Festivals and Events in Arizona

As the cannabis industry continues to grow in Arizona, so too does the number of cannabis-related festivals and events. These gatherings provide a platform for cannabis enthusiasts, industry professionals, and advocates to come together and celebrate the state's emerging cannabis culture.

One of the most anticipated events is the Phoenix Cannabis Expo, which brings together cannabis businesses, entrepreneurs, and consumers for a weekend of networking, product showcases, and educational panels. The expo provides valuable insights into the latest trends and innovations in the cannabis industry, making it a must-attend event for anyone involved in the market.

Another major event is the Arizona 420 Festival, a celebration of cannabis culture that features live music, food vendors, and educational workshops on topics such as cannabis law, cultivation, and wellness. The festival has become one of the state's premier cannabis events, drawing attendees from across the Southwest.

In addition to these larger events, Arizona is home to a variety of cannabis-friendly pop-up markets, yoga classes, and infused dining experiences. These events often focus on specific aspects of cannabis culture, such as cannabis-infused cooking or CBD-based wellness practices, providing attendees with an opportunity to explore the many ways cannabis can enhance their lives.

Challenges and Opportunities in Arizona's Cannabis Market

Arizona's cannabis industry has experienced rapid growth since the legalization of recreational cannabis, but it also faces several challenges, particularly in terms of regulatory compliance and taxation. The state's strict regulations around product testing, security, and advertising have made it difficult for some businesses to operate, particularly smaller companies that may not have the resources to meet these requirements.

Another challenge is the high taxes on cannabis products, which can make legal cannabis more expensive than products available on the black market. This has led to concerns about the sustainability of the legal market, particularly in rural areas where consumers may be more likely to turn to illegal sources for cannabis.

Despite these challenges, Arizona's cannabis industry offers significant opportunities for growth, particularly in areas such as cannabis tourism, sustainable cultivation, and wellness retreats. As the state continues to refine its regulatory framework and expand its social equity programs, Arizona is poised to become a leader in the national cannabis market, offering a unique blend of outdoor adventure, luxury experiences, and wellness-focused cannabis culture.

Chapter 14: Virginia - Pioneering Cannabis Reform in the South

Virginia made history in 2021 by becoming the first Southern state to legalize recreational cannabis, setting a powerful precedent for cannabis reform in the region. The passage of the Virginia Cannabis Control Act marked a monumental shift in a state traditionally known for its conservative politics. This move places Virginia at the forefront of cannabis reform in the South and has ignited conversations about legalization in neighboring states. With its blend of urban centers like Richmond, Northern Virginia, and rural communities stretching to the Appalachian Mountains, Virginia's cannabis culture is poised for a unique evolution.

As the state moves toward full legalization with dispensaries and retail operations set to begin in the coming years, Virginia is embracing cannabis as part of its economic and social future. The state's commitment to social equity, racial justice, and public health are key components of its approach, and Virginia's cannabis market could become one of the most progressive and inclusive in the country.

The Path to Legalization in Virginia

The legalization of recreational cannabis in Virginia was the culmination of years of advocacy and political momentum. In April 2021, Virginia lawmakers passed the Virginia Cannabis Control Act, legalizing the possession and personal cultivation of cannabis for adults over the age of 21. The law also set a timeline for the development of a legal cannabis marketplace, with sales expected to begin in 2024. This delay in retail sales gives the state time to establish a regulatory framework and ensure the market is set up for long-term success.

One of the most significant aspects of Virginia's legalization law is its focus on social equity and racial justice. Like many other states, Virginia's law includes provisions to expunge past cannabis convictions and prioritize licenses for individuals from communities disproportionately impacted by the war on drugs. These efforts are designed to create a more inclusive cannabis industry and address the racial disparities in cannabis-related arrests and incarceration.

Virginia's approach to legalization is also notable for its emphasis on public health and consumer safety. The state's law includes strict regulations around product testing, labeling, and advertising to ensure that all cannabis products sold in the state are safe and of high quality. These regulations are intended to protect consumers and create a responsible cannabis marketplace that prioritizes public health.

Cannabis Culture in Virginia's Major Cities

As Virginia's cannabis industry develops, cities like Richmond, Charlottesville, and Northern Virginia are becoming hubs for cannabis culture and commerce. In Richmond, the state's capital, cannabis is beginning to make its mark on the local arts and food scenes, with chefs, artists, and entrepreneurs exploring the potential of cannabis as part of the city's creative economy.

Richmond's rich history and vibrant cultural scene make it an ideal location for cannabis-infused dining experiences, where chefs collaborate with local cannabis producers to create multi-course meals that highlight Virginia's culinary traditions. These dinners often take place at private venues or pop-up restaurants, offering an exclusive and intimate dining experience for cannabis enthusiasts. Many of these meals are paired with cannabis-infused cocktails or mocktails, allowing diners to enjoy cannabis in a controlled and sophisticated setting.

In Charlottesville, home to the University of Virginia, cannabis is becoming part of the city's progressive and college-town culture. The city's young population, combined with its focus on health and wellness, has created a growing demand for cannabis wellness products, including CBD-infused creams, oils, and edibles. Charlottesville's farmers' markets are also beginning to feature locally produced hemp and CBD products, further integrating cannabis into the local economy.

Northern Virginia, with its proximity to Washington, D.C., is also embracing cannabis culture, particularly in cities like Arlington and Alexandria. As dispensaries begin to open in the coming years, Northern Virginia is expected to become a major market for cannabis retail, attracting both local consumers and tourists from the D.C. metropolitan area. The region's diverse population and affluent communities make it an ideal location for high-end dispensaries and cannabis-friendly businesses.

Cannabis Tourism in Virginia

Virginia's rich history, scenic landscapes, and proximity to major cities make it an attractive destination for cannabis tourism. As the state's cannabis industry develops, tourists will be able to explore Virginia's dispensaries, cannabis-friendly accommodations, and outdoor adventures while enjoying the state's unique blend of history and natural beauty.

One of the most popular attractions for cannabis tourists is expected to be the cannabis-friendly bed-and-breakfasts located in Virginia's wine country. These accommodations offer a relaxed and luxurious experience for guests, with cannabis-friendly amenities such as designated smoking areas, cannabis-infused spa treatments, and curated cannabis experiences that highlight Virginia's agricultural heritage. Many of these bed-and-breakfasts are located near Virginia's wineries and breweries, allowing guests to enjoy both cannabis and local craft beverages in a scenic and tranquil setting.

For those looking to combine cannabis with outdoor activities, Virginia offers cannabis-friendly retreats in the Blue Ridge Mountains and along the Appalachian Trail. These retreats often feature activities like yoga, meditation, hiking, and spa treatments, providing participants with a holistic and wellness-focused cannabis experience. Cannabis enthusiasts can enjoy the state's natural beauty while exploring the wellness benefits of cannabis in a serene and peaceful environment.

In addition to wellness retreats, Virginia is expected to see the rise of cannabis tours, which take visitors on guided journeys through the state's dispensaries, grow facilities, and cannabis-related attractions. These tours will provide an insider's look at Virginia's cannabis industry, with stops at historic landmarks and scenic locations along the way.

Cannabis and Virginia's Food Culture

Virginia has a rich culinary history, and cannabis is beginning to make its mark on the state's food scene. From cannabis-infused dinners to CBD-based wellness products, Virginia's chefs and food producers are exploring the possibilities of incorporating cannabis into their menus and products.

In Richmond, chefs are collaborating with local cannabis producers to create cannabis-infused multi-course meals that highlight Virginia's farm-to-table traditions. These dinners often feature dishes infused with low doses of THC or CBD, allowing diners to enjoy the effects of cannabis without becoming overly intoxicated. Many of these meals are paired with Virginia wines and craft beers, creating a full sensory experience that celebrates both cannabis and Virginia's agricultural heritage.

Charlottesville's vibrant food scene is also beginning to incorporate cannabis, with local producers offering CBD-infused oils, honeys, and baked goods at farmers' markets and health food stores. These products are popular among health-conscious consumers who are interested in the wellness benefits of cannabis without the psychoactive effects of THC.

Challenges and Opportunities in Virginia's Cannabis Market

While Virginia's cannabis industry holds significant promise, the state faces several challenges as it moves toward full legalization. One of the biggest challenges is the delay in retail sales, with legal sales not expected to begin until 2024. This has created uncertainty for businesses and consumers, as the state works to establish a regulatory framework and licensing process for dispensaries.

Another challenge is the high cost of entry into the cannabis market, particularly for small businesses and entrepreneurs. The state's licensing fees and regulatory requirements are expected to be stringent, making it difficult for some businesses to compete with larger, well-funded companies. However, Virginia's social equity programs, which prioritize licenses for individuals from communities disproportionately impacted by cannabis prohibition, are designed to help level the playing field and create a more inclusive market.

Despite these challenges, Virginia's cannabis industry offers significant opportunities for growth, particularly in areas such as cannabis tourism, social consumption lounges, and sustainable cultivation. As the state continues to refine its regulatory framework and expand its social equity programs, Virginia is poised to become a leader in the national cannabis market, offering a unique blend of history, culture, and wellness-focused cannabis experiences.

Chapter 15: Texas - The Fight for Cannabis Reform in the Lone Star State

Texas is one of the largest and most influential states in the United States, and its path toward cannabis reform has been slow but steadily progressing. While recreational cannabis remains illegal in Texas, the state has made strides in expanding access to medical cannabis through its Compassionate Use Program, which allows patients with certain qualifying medical conditions to access low-THC cannabis products. However, the fight for full legalization continues to gain momentum, with advocates pushing for broader cannabis reform in the Lone Star State.

The sheer size and diversity of Texas create a unique landscape for cannabis reform, with urban centers like Austin, Houston, Dallas, and San Antonio showing strong support for legalization, while rural areas remain more conservative. Despite the political challenges, Texas has a vibrant cannabis culture that is beginning to emerge, driven by grassroots activism, medical cannabis patients, and a growing wellness movement.

The Compassionate Use Program: Medical Cannabis in Texas

Texas' Compassionate Use Program was first established in 2015, allowing patients with severe epilepsy to access low-THC cannabis oil. Since then, the program has expanded to include more qualifying conditions, such as PTSD, chronic pain, and multiple sclerosis, but it remains one of the most restrictive medical cannabis programs in the country. Under the current law, patients can only access cannabis products with a THC content of 1% or less, limiting the options available to those who could benefit from higher-THC products.

Despite these restrictions, the Compassionate Use Program has provided relief to thousands of patients across Texas, and the demand for medical cannabis continues to grow. Dispensaries licensed under the program offer a range of products, including tinctures, capsules, and topicals, all designed to help patients manage their symptoms without the psychoactive effects of high-THC cannabis. However, the limited nature of the program has led many patients to seek alternative treatments or travel to states with more expansive medical cannabis programs.

Advocates for cannabis reform in Texas are pushing to expand the Compassionate Use Program further, with efforts to increase the allowable THC content and broaden the list of qualifying conditions. These efforts are seen as a critical step toward full legalization, as public opinion in Texas continues to shift in favor of broader access to cannabis.

Grassroots Activism and the Push for Legalization

Texas' journey toward cannabis reform has been fueled by a passionate community of activists, patients, and advocates who are working tirelessly to change the state's cannabis laws. Organizations like Texas NORML and Marijuana Policy Project have played a leading role in advocating for legalization, organizing rallies, educational events, and lobbying efforts at the state capitol.

One of the most notable victories for cannabis reform in Texas came in 2019, when the state passed a law decriminalizing small amounts of cannabis. Under the new law, individuals caught with less than four ounces of cannabis are no longer subject to arrest or jail time, and instead face a fine or civil penalty. This change in policy has been a significant step toward reducing the number of cannabis-related arrests in Texas, particularly in cities like Austin and Houston, where local law enforcement has prioritized decriminalization.

Despite this progress, full legalization remains a contentious issue in Texas, with opposition from conservative lawmakers and influential interest groups. However, the fight for legalization is gaining momentum, with polls showing that a majority of Texans now support the legalization of recreational cannabis. As more states across the country move toward legalization, many believe that Texas will eventually follow suit, driven by economic opportunity, public health benefits, and shifting political dynamics.

Cannabis Culture in Texas' Major Cities

While recreational cannabis remains illegal in Texas, a vibrant cannabis culture is emerging in the state's major cities, particularly in Austin, Houston, Dallas, and San Antonio. Each of these cities has its own unique approach to cannabis, reflecting the diversity of Texas' population and regional differences.

Austin, the state's capital and known for its progressive culture, has become a hub for cannabis advocacy and wellness. The city is home to a growing number of CBD shops, wellness retreats, and cannabis-friendly events that cater to health-conscious consumers. Austin's creative community has also embraced cannabis, with local artists, musicians, and chefs incorporating cannabis into their work through art shows, live performances, and cannabis-infused dinners.

Houston, the largest city in Texas, has a more conservative reputation, but cannabis culture is beginning to take root in the city's diverse neighborhoods. Dispensaries licensed under the Compassionate Use Program are becoming more common, and CBD-based wellness products are widely available at health food stores, cafes, and farmers' markets. Houston's culinary scene is also exploring the potential of CBD-infused dishes and beverages, offering diners a unique way to experience cannabis as part of the city's rich food culture.

In Dallas and San Antonio, cannabis culture is still developing, but both cities have seen an increase in CBD shops, wellness events, and cannabis-friendly businesses. Dallas, with its growing tech scene and young population, is beginning to embrace cannabis as part of the city's health and wellness movement. San Antonio, known for its strong military presence, has seen a rise in demand for medical cannabis among veterans, many of whom are advocating for expanded access to cannabis as a treatment for PTSD and other service-related conditions.

The Future of Cannabis Legalization in Texas

While the road to full legalization in Texas may be longer than in other states, the potential for growth is enormous. Texas' large population, diverse economy, and agricultural capacity make it an ideal state for the development of a robust cannabis industry. Many believe that if Texas were to legalize recreational cannabis, the state could become one of the largest cannabis markets in the country, attracting businesses, investors, and consumers from across the region.

One of the key drivers for legalization in Texas is the potential for economic growth. Legalizing cannabis could generate billions of dollars in tax revenue, create thousands of jobs, and provide a significant boost to the state's economy. Additionally, legalization could help reduce the state's reliance on the criminal justice system to address cannabis-related offenses, freeing up resources for more pressing public safety issues.

Another factor driving the push for legalization is the increasing demand for cannabis tourism in Texas. Cities like Austin, Houston, and Dallas are already popular destinations for visitors, and the addition of a legal cannabis market could attract even more tourists interested in exploring the state's cannabis culture. Cannabis-friendly hotels, tours, and events could become a major draw for visitors, boosting the state's tourism industry and providing new opportunities for local businesses.

Cannabis and Texas' Agricultural Potential

Texas is known for its vast agricultural resources, and the state's farmers are beginning to explore the potential of cannabis cultivation as a new and profitable crop. While hemp cultivation has been legal in Texas since 2019, the state's climate and soil conditions are well-suited for cannabis cultivation, and many believe that Texas could become a major producer of both hemp and cannabis if recreational legalization is achieved.

Texas' agricultural communities, particularly in West Texas and the Rio Grande Valley, have expressed interest in cultivating cannabis as a way to diversify their crops and boost the state's agricultural economy. The state's farmers are already experienced in growing a variety of crops, from cotton to pecans, and many believe that cannabis could be a valuable addition to Texas' agricultural portfolio.

Challenges and Opportunities in Texas' Cannabis Market

Despite the growing demand for cannabis reform, Texas faces several challenges in achieving full legalization. One of the biggest obstacles is the state's conservative political climate, with many lawmakers and influential interest groups opposing legalization efforts. Additionally, Texas' large size and regional differences create logistical challenges for implementing a statewide cannabis market, particularly in rural areas where opposition to cannabis remains strong.

However, the opportunities for growth in Texas' cannabis market are significant. The state's large population, strong economy, and agricultural capacity make it an ideal candidate for a thriving cannabis industry. As public opinion continues to shift and neighboring states move toward legalization, many believe that Texas will eventually follow suit, creating one of the largest and most diverse cannabis markets in the country.

Chapter 16: Vermont - Leading the Charge for Craft Cannabis in New England

Vermont, with its picturesque landscapes and progressive policies, has emerged as a key player in the cannabis industry of New England. Known for its focus on small-scale, sustainable agriculture, Vermont has taken a different approach to cannabis legalization, prioritizing craft cannabis and local, artisanal production. In 2018, Vermont became the first state to legalize cannabis through legislative action, and while its cannabis market is smaller than those of other states, it has cultivated a reputation for high-quality, organic cannabis products.

Vermont's cannabis culture is deeply rooted in its traditions of self-reliance, community engagement, and environmental responsibility. With cities like Burlington and Montpelier at the forefront, Vermont's cannabis market is growing steadily, emphasizing organic farming, sustainability, and support for small businesses. While Vermont is not known for large-scale cannabis production, its focus on craft cultivation and environmental stewardship makes it a leader in the artisanal cannabis movement.

Vermont's Unique Approach to Legalization

Vermont's cannabis legalization process was notably different from other states, as it was the first state to legalize cannabis for recreational use through a legislative vote, rather than a ballot initiative. In 2018, the Vermont Legislature passed a law allowing adults over the age of 21 to possess and grow small amounts of cannabis for personal use. The law, however, did not initially create a regulatory framework for the sale of cannabis, which meant that Vermont residents could cultivate and consume cannabis but could not purchase it from legal dispensaries.

In 2020, Vermont's legislature took further action, passing a law that established a regulated market for cannabis sales. This law set the stage for the creation of licensed dispensaries and producers, with a strong emphasis on supporting small-scale growers and local businesses. Vermont's cannabis regulations focus on sustainability, organic farming practices, and social equity, ensuring that the state's cannabis market aligns with its broader environmental and community values.

One of the unique aspects of Vermont's cannabis laws is the state's encouragement of small-scale cultivation. Unlike states that have allowed large corporate entities to dominate the cannabis market, Vermont has focused on promoting craft cannabis producers, giving preference to small, local farmers who practice organic and sustainable farming techniques. This approach has helped Vermont build a cannabis industry that reflects the state's commitment to environmental responsibility and community-based agriculture.

The Dispensary Scene in Vermont

While Vermont's recreational cannabis market is still in its early stages, the state has a growing number of medical dispensaries that serve both medical patients and, in some cases, recreational consumers. Dispensaries in Vermont often emphasize locally sourced, organic products, reflecting the state's focus on craft cannabis and sustainability.

In Burlington, the state's largest city, dispensaries like Champlain Valley Dispensary and Grassroots Vermont are known for their high-quality, locally grown cannabis products. These dispensaries offer a variety of products, including flower, edibles, concentrates, and tinctures, many of which are produced by small-scale, organic farmers from the region. Burlington's dispensaries also prioritize customer education, providing resources on safe cannabis consumption, dosing, and product selection.

Vermont's dispensaries often focus on wellness-oriented experiences, with many offering products that cater to health-conscious consumers. CBD-rich products, such as oils, topicals, and edibles, are particularly popular in Vermont, as they appeal to individuals looking for the therapeutic benefits of cannabis without the psychoactive effects of THC. Dispensaries in Vermont also offer a range of THC-infused products, including tinctures, capsules, and topicals designed to promote relaxation, pain relief, and overall well-being.

Craft Cannabis and Sustainability in Vermont

Vermont's focus on craft cannabis and sustainable cultivation sets it apart from other states in the cannabis industry. The state's emphasis on small-batch production, organic farming, and environmental responsibility reflects Vermont's broader commitment to sustainable agriculture and community-based farming practices.

Many of Vermont's cannabis growers use organic farming techniques, avoiding the use of synthetic pesticides, herbicides, and fertilizers. Instead, they rely on natural soil amendments, composting, and integrated pest management to cultivate high-quality cannabis that is free from harmful chemicals. Vermont's growers also focus on sun-grown cannabis, taking advantage of the state's natural growing conditions to produce cannabis with a low environmental footprint.

The state's small-batch approach to cannabis cultivation allows growers to focus on the quality of their product rather than mass production. This artisanal approach has helped Vermont develop a reputation for premium craft cannabis, with many of the state's products sought after by consumers who prioritize quality, flavor, and environmental responsibility.

Vermont's commitment to sustainability extends beyond the cultivation process, with many cannabis businesses in the state adopting green business practices. These include the use of recyclable packaging, energy-efficient lighting, and water conservation techniques. Vermont's cannabis industry is also exploring the use of solar energy and other renewable energy sources to power cultivation facilities, further reducing the industry's environmental impact.

Cannabis Culture in Vermont's Major Cities

Vermont's cannabis culture is closely tied to the state's progressive values and emphasis on wellness, sustainability, and community engagement. In cities like Burlington and Montpelier, cannabis has become an integral part of the local culture, with cannabis-friendly businesses, events, and wellness practices becoming more common.

Burlington, home to the University of Vermont, has embraced cannabis as part of its wellness and outdoor recreation culture. The city's dispensaries often focus on providing products that promote relaxation, pain relief, and overall well-being. Cannabis-infused yoga classes and wellness workshops are becoming popular in Burlington, offering residents and visitors a chance to explore the therapeutic benefits of cannabis in a peaceful and supportive environment.

Montpelier, Vermont's capital city, has also embraced cannabis as part of its wellness culture. The city's focus on health and sustainability is reflected in its dispensaries, many of which offer a variety of CBD products, organic edibles, and THC-infused topicals. Montpelier's small-town charm and emphasis on local business make it an ideal location for craft cannabis producers and retailers.

Cannabis Tourism in Vermont

Vermont's stunning natural landscapes and commitment to sustainability make it a popular destination for cannabis tourism. With its scenic mountains, forests, and rivers, Vermont offers a variety of outdoor activities that can be enjoyed alongside cannabis consumption. Cannabis-friendly bed-and-breakfasts and wellness retreats are becoming increasingly popular in Vermont, providing tourists with an opportunity to relax and unwind while enjoying the state's natural beauty.

One of the most popular attractions for cannabis tourists is the cannabis farm tour, which takes visitors on a guided journey through some of Vermont's best small-scale, organic cannabis farms. These tours often include stops at sun-grown cultivation sites, where tourists can learn about the growing process, meet local far, and sample fresh cannabis products. Many tours also offer workshops on sustainable farming practices, giving visitors an in-depth look at Vermont's commitment to environmentally friendly cannabis cultivation.

For those looking to combine cannabis with wellness, Vermont offers a growing number of cannabis-friendly wellness retreats in scenic locations like the Green Mountains and the Northeast Kingdom. These retreats often feature activities like yoga, meditation, and hiking, allowing participants to enjoy cannabis in a serene and rejuvenating environment. Cannabis-infused spa treatments and gourmet dinners are also popular offerings at many of Vermont's wellness retreats, providing tourists with a luxurious and relaxing cannabis experience.

Challenges and Opportunities in Vermont's Cannabis Market

While Vermont's cannabis market is growing, the state faces several challenges, particularly in terms of market size and competition. Vermont's relatively small population means that the state's cannabis market is not as large as those of other states, which can make it difficult for businesses to scale. Additionally, Vermont's focus on small-scale cultivation means that it may be more challenging for businesses to compete with larger, corporate cannabis producers in other states.

However, Vermont's emphasis on craft cannabis and sustainability presents significant opportunities for growth, particularly in the areas of cannabis tourism and wellness products. As more consumers become interested in high-quality, organic cannabis, Vermont is well-positioned to become a leader in the premium cannabis market. The state's focus on small-batch production and environmental responsibility appeals to consumers who value ethically produced products and are willing to pay a premium for cannabis that is grown with care.

The Future of Cannabis in Vermont

Looking ahead, Vermont's cannabis industry is expected to continue growing, with an emphasis on supporting small-scale producers and promoting sustainable business practices. The state's commitment to social equity and environmental responsibility sets it apart from other cannabis markets, and its focus on craft cannabis makes it a unique destination for consumers looking for premium, artisanal products.

As Vermont's cannabis industry matures, the state is likely to see an increase in cannabis tourism, wellness products, and organic cannabis cultivation. Vermont's small but passionate community of cannabis entrepreneurs, advocates, and consumers will continue to play a key role in shaping the future of cannabis in the state and beyond.

Chapter 17: Georgia - An Emerging Medical Cannabis Market

Georgia's cannabis reform journey has been slow compared to other states, but recent efforts have laid the foundation for a medical cannabis program that could grow significantly in the coming years. In 2015, Georgia passed the Haleigh's Hope Act, which allowed patients with certain conditions to legally possess low-THC cannabis oil. However, it wasn't until 2019, with the passage of the Georgia's Hope Act, that the state created a framework for in-state production and distribution of low-THC oil to qualifying patients.

Despite its limitations, Georgia's medical cannabis program is slowly expanding, and cities like Atlanta, Savannah, and Augusta are becoming hubs of advocacy and patient care. As Georgia's medical cannabis industry develops, there is growing support for broader reforms, including the expansion of the state's medical program and the potential legalization of recreational cannabis in the future.

Haleigh's Hope Act and Georgia's Hope Act: Legalizing Low-THC Oil

Georgia's medical cannabis journey began in 2015 with the passage of the Haleigh's Hope Act, which allowed patients with qualifying conditions to possess low-THC cannabis oil (containing no more than 5% THC) for therapeutic use. The law was named after Haleigh Cox, a young girl who suffered from severe epilepsy and whose case became a symbol of the fight for medical cannabis in Georgia.

The law initially allowed only a limited number of conditions to qualify for cannabis oil treatment, including seizure disorders, Crohn's disease, multiple sclerosis, and Parkinson's disease. However, patients were unable to legally purchase or grow cannabis in the state, as Georgia did not provide a system for in-state cultivation or distribution. This created a legal gray area for patients, who could possess low-THC oil but had no legal way to obtain it.

In 2019, Georgia addressed this issue with the passage of the Georgia's Hope Act, which created a regulated system for the production and distribution of low-THC oil within the state. The law established a licensing framework for cannabis oil producers and authorized the creation of state-licensed dispensaries, allowing patients to legally purchase low-THC oil from licensed providers. The law also expanded the list of qualifying conditions to include PTSD, autism, and terminal cancer.

Despite these advancements, Georgia's medical cannabis program remains highly restrictive. Only low-THC oil is permitted, and the state's licensing process for producers and dispensaries has been slow to roll out. However, the passage of the Georgia's Hope Act has given patients a legal pathway to access the medicine they need, and advocates continue to push for broader reforms that would allow for full-strength medical cannabis and an expansion of the state's qualifying conditions.

The Dispensary Scene in Georgia

Georgia's medical cannabis program is still in its early stages, and the state has only recently begun issuing licenses for cannabis oil producers and dispensaries. As a result, the dispensary scene in Georgia is limited, with only a few licensed dispensaries expected to open in the coming years. These dispensaries will offer low-THC oil products to patients with qualifying conditions, providing much-needed access to medical cannabis in a state that has historically been resistant to cannabis reform.

One of the challenges facing Georgia's dispensary market is the state's strict limitations on THC content, which prevent dispensaries from offering full-spectrum cannabis products. However, as more patients begin using low-THC oil for their medical conditions, there is growing support for expanding the state's cannabis program to include higher-THC products and a broader range of delivery methods.

In addition to the state's emerging dispensary market, Georgia is home to a growing number of CBD retailers, which offer a wide variety of hemp-derived CBD products that are legal under federal law. These products include CBD tinctures, edibles, topicals, and vape products, and they have become popular among Georgians seeking natural remedies for conditions like anxiety, pain, and inflammation.

Cannabis Culture in Georgia's Major Cities

While Georgia's cannabis laws remain restrictive, the state's cannabis culture is slowly emerging, particularly in cities like Atlanta, Savannah, and Augusta, where advocates and patients are working to expand access to medical cannabis and raise awareness about the therapeutic benefits of cannabis.

Atlanta, the state's capital and largest city, has become a hub for cannabis advocacy and patient care. The city is home to a number of CBD shops, wellness centers, and cannabis-friendly businesses that cater to health-conscious consumers and medical cannabis patients. Atlanta's progressive attitude toward cannabis, combined with its role as a cultural and political center, has made it a focal point for efforts to expand Georgia's medical cannabis program and push for broader cannabis reform.

Savannah, a historic coastal city known for its vibrant arts scene and tourism industry, has also seen growing support for cannabis reform. Dispensaries in Savannah will soon offer low-THC oil products to patients with qualifying conditions, and the city's residents are increasingly turning to CBD products for relief from a variety of health issues. Savannah's cannabis culture is closely tied to its focus on wellness and natural health, with many local businesses offering CBD-based therapies and holistic treatments.

In Augusta, home to the famous Masters Golf Tournament, cannabis culture is slowly gaining traction as more residents become aware of the potential benefits of medical cannabis. Dispensaries in Augusta will provide patients with access to low-THC oil for the treatment of conditions like chronic pain and epilepsy, and the city's growing number of CBD retailers offer a range of products designed to promote health and well-being.

Cannabis Tourism in Georgia

Given Georgia's limited medical cannabis program, cannabis tourism is still in its early stages. However, the state's CBD market and hemp industry are attracting interest from tourists seeking wellness experiences and natural remedies. Cities like Atlanta and Savannah are home to a growing number of CBD-friendly wellness retreats, spas, and yoga studios, which incorporate cannabis into their services to promote relaxation and holistic healing.

One of the most popular destinations for cannabis tourists is Savannah, where visitors can explore the city's CBD shops and wellness centers while enjoying its historic charm and coastal beauty. Savannah's growing wellness tourism industry, combined with its progressive attitude toward cannabis, makes it an ideal destination for those interested in exploring Georgia's emerging cannabis culture.

As Georgia's medical cannabis program expands, the state's tourism industry may benefit from an increase in medical cannabis patients traveling to Georgia to access low-THC oil products. Additionally, the state's hemp farming industry could become a draw for visitors interested in learning about the cultivation and processing of hemp-derived products.

Cannabis Festivals and Events in Georgia

As Georgia's cannabis industry continues to develop, the state is seeing a growing number of hemp and CBD-themed festivals, expos, and events that celebrate the state's evolving cannabis market. One of the most well-known events is the Georgia Hemp & CBD Expo, which takes place annually in Atlanta and brings together industry professionals, patients, and advocates for a weekend of education, networking, and product showcases.

Another popular event is the Southern Hemp Expo, which focuses on the future of the hemp industry in Georgia and the broader southeastern United States. The expo features educational panels, product displays, and workshops on the latest trends and developments in the hemp and CBD markets, making it a valuable resource for anyone involved in the industry.

In addition to these larger events, Georgia is home to a growing number of CBD-friendly wellness seminars, yoga retreats, and pop-up markets that promote the health benefits of CBD and hemp-derived products. These smaller, more intimate events provide consumers with an opportunity to explore the diverse ways in which cannabis can be incorporated into everyday life, from holistic treatments to natural health remedies.

Challenges and Opportunities in Georgia's Cannabis Market

While Georgia's cannabis market is still in its infancy, the state faces several challenges, particularly in terms of regulatory barriers and market access. Georgia's medical cannabis program remains highly restrictive, limiting access to low-THC oil and excluding many patients who could benefit from full-spectrum cannabis products.

Another challenge facing Georgia's cannabis market is the slow rollout of the state's dispensary licensing process. While the Georgia's Hope Act created a framework for in-state production and distribution of low-THC oil, the licensing process for cannabis producers and dispensaries has been slow to develop, leaving many patients without access to the medicine they need.

Despite these challenges, Georgia's cannabis industry offers significant opportunities for growth, particularly in the areas of medical cannabis and CBD product development. As more patients become aware of the therapeutic benefits of cannabis, there is growing support for expanding the state's medical cannabis program and eventually legalizing recreational cannabis.

The Future of Cannabis in Georgia

The future of cannabis in Georgia is full of potential, with the state's growing medical cannabis program and CBD market paving the way for further reform. As more patients seek out cannabis-based therapies, advocates will continue to push for broader access to medical cannabis, including higher-THC products and a wider range of delivery methods.

As public support for cannabis reform grows, there is hope that Georgia will eventually join the ranks of states that have legalized recreational cannabis, creating new economic opportunities and increasing access to cannabis for residents across the state. The expansion of Georgia's medical cannabis program and the potential legalization of recreational cannabis could have a significant impact on the state's economy, particularly in terms of job creation, tax revenue, and business development.

In the near future, Georgia's cannabis industry is expected to grow as more patients enroll in the state's medical cannabis program and new dispensaries begin to open. With its emphasis on low-THC oil and patient care, Georgia's medical cannabis market is likely to continue focusing on the therapeutic benefits of cannabis for those suffering from chronic pain, seizure disorders, and other qualifying conditions.

At the same time, the state's CBD market and hemp industry will continue to expand, offering opportunities for local farmers, entrepreneurs, and retailers to capitalize on the growing demand for hemp-derived products. Georgia's favorable climate for hemp cultivation, combined with its large population and strong agricultural base, positions the state as a potential leader in the national hemp market.

Looking ahead, the future of cannabis in Georgia will depend on continued advocacy efforts and changes in public opinion. As more Georgians experience the health benefits of cannabis, the state may move toward broader cannabis reform, including the legalization of recreational cannabis. If Georgia fully embraces cannabis legalization, it could unlock new economic opportunities, provide greater access to cannabis for patients and consumers, and position the state as a major player in the U.S. cannabis industry.

Chapter 18: North Carolina - The Road to Cannabis Reform in the Tar Heel State

North Carolina is one of the states where cannabis reform has been slower to take root compared to others in the Southeast. While the state has made some progress in legalizing hemp and CBD products, North Carolina has yet to establish a comprehensive medical cannabis program, and recreational cannabis remains illegal. Despite these challenges, support for cannabis reform is growing among the state's residents, and advocates are pushing for changes that would allow patients greater access to medical cannabis.

North Carolina's cannabis landscape is shaped by the state's strong agricultural heritage, progressive urban centers like Charlotte, Raleigh, and Asheville, and a growing demand for natural health remedies. As more residents become aware of the therapeutic benefits of cannabis and hemp-derived products, the push for cannabis legalization is expected to gain momentum.

Hemp and CBD in North Carolina

North Carolina has been at the forefront of the hemp industry since the passage of the 2014 federal Farm Bill, which allowed for the legal cultivation of hemp for research purposes. In 2017, the state passed legislation that created a legal framework for hemp farming, making North Carolina one of the leading hemp producers in the Southeast. The state's climate and agricultural resources make it an ideal location for hemp cultivation, and North Carolina farmers have capitalized on this by growing hemp for use in CBD products and industrial applications.

The state's hemp and CBD market has grown rapidly in recent years, with CBD shops, wellness centers, and hemp farms cropping up across the state. These businesses offer a wide range of CBD-based products, including tinctures, topicals, edibles, and vape cartridges, catering to consumers seeking natural remedies for conditions like anxiety, pain, and inflammation. North Carolina's CBD market has become a thriving industry, particularly in cities like Asheville, known for its progressive and wellness-focused community.

The success of the hemp industry in North Carolina has helped normalize cannabis use, and many residents are hopeful that the state will eventually expand access to medical cannabis. Advocates continue to push for a comprehensive medical cannabis program, which they argue would provide patients with a safe and legal way to access cannabis for therapeutic purposes.

Cannabis Advocacy in North Carolina

While North Carolina's cannabis laws remain restrictive, the state is home to a growing number of cannabis advocacy groups that are working to change public opinion and push for cannabis reform. Organizations like NC NORML (National Organization for the Reform of Marijuana Laws) and the North Carolina Cannabis Patients Network have been at the forefront of efforts to educate lawmakers and the public about the benefits of medical cannabis.

Advocates in North Carolina are focused on creating a medical cannabis program that would allow patients with conditions like chronic pain, epilepsy, cancer, and PTSD to access cannabis products for relief. Many believe that the success of the state's hemp and CBD industry could pave the way for broader cannabis reform, particularly as more residents become familiar with the therapeutic benefits of cannabis.

In addition to advocating for medical cannabis, activists are also pushing for decriminalization and the eventual legalization of recreational cannabis. Although recreational legalization may be further off in North Carolina, growing public support and changing political attitudes could eventually lead to significant policy changes.

Cannabis Culture in North Carolina's Major Cities

North Carolina's cannabis culture is still in its early stages, but cities like Asheville, Charlotte, and Raleigh are leading the way in fostering a growing community of cannabis advocates, patients, and entrepreneurs. These cities are known for their progressive attitudes, focus on wellness, and support for natural health remedies, making them ideal locations for the state's emerging cannabis culture.

Asheville, nestled in the Blue Ridge Mountains, has long been known for its thriving arts scene and emphasis on holistic living. The city is home to a number of CBD shops, wellness centers, and cannabis-friendly businesses that cater to health-conscious consumers seeking natural alternatives to traditional medicine. Asheville's residents have been at the forefront of efforts to expand access to medical cannabis, and the city's cannabis culture is closely tied to its focus on community health and well-being.

Charlotte, the state's largest city, is also seeing growing support for cannabis reform. The city's residents have embraced CBD products for their therapeutic benefits, and local businesses are capitalizing on the demand for natural health remedies. Charlotte is home to a growing number of CBD retailers and wellness centers, which offer products and services designed to promote relaxation and holistic healing. As more residents become familiar with the benefits of CBD and hemp-derived products, support for cannabis reform in Charlotte is expected to increase.

In Raleigh, North Carolina's capital, cannabis culture is slowly emerging as more residents advocate for the legalization of medical cannabis. Dispensaries that sell hemp-derived products are gaining popularity in the city, and the growing number of wellness-oriented businesses reflects Raleigh's focus on promoting the health benefits of natural remedies. As the state's political center, Raleigh plays an important role in shaping cannabis policy, and local advocates are working to influence lawmakers to push for broader cannabis reform.

Cannabis Tourism in North Carolina

North Carolina's CBD market and hemp industry are attracting growing interest from tourists seeking wellness experiences and natural health remedies. Cities like Asheville and Wilmington are popular destinations for tourists looking to explore the state's scenic beauty while enjoying the benefits of CBD-based products and holistic wellness practices.

One of the most popular destinations for cannabis tourists in North Carolina is Asheville, where visitors can enjoy CBD-infused massages, hemp-friendly yoga classes, and wellness retreats that focus on promoting relaxation and healing through the use of hemp-derived products. Asheville's thriving hemp culture and its emphasis on holistic health make it an ideal destination for those interested in exploring the potential benefits of cannabis.

In addition to Asheville, cities like Wilmington and Greensboro are seeing a rise in hemp-based businesses and CBD-friendly events. Tourists visiting these cities can explore local CBD shops, hemp farms, and wellness centers, offering a unique way to experience North Carolina's evolving cannabis culture.

Cannabis Festivals and Events in North Carolina

As North Carolina's cannabis industry continues to develop, the state is seeing a growing number of hemp and CBD-themed festivals, expos, and educational events that celebrate the state's emerging cannabis market. One of the most well-known events is the Asheville Hemp Fest, which brings together hemp farmers, CBD entrepreneurs, and cannabis advocates for a weekend of music, education, and community engagement.

Another major event is the Southeast Cannabis Conference and Expo, which takes place annually in Charlotte and focuses on the future of the hemp and cannabis industries in North Carolina and the broader Southeast. The conference features educational panels, product displays, and networking opportunities for industry professionals, patients, and advocates interested in the latest trends and developments in the cannabis market.

In addition to these larger events, North Carolina is home to a growing number of CBD-friendly pop-up markets, wellness retreats, and educational workshops that promote the health benefits of hemp and cannabis. These events provide consumers with an opportunity to learn more about the therapeutic uses of cannabis and connect with others in the community.

Challenges and Opportunities in North Carolina's Cannabis Market

While North Carolina's cannabis market is still in its early stages, the state faces several challenges, particularly in terms of regulatory barriers and limited access to cannabis products. The lack of a comprehensive medical cannabis program prevents many patients from accessing cannabis for therapeutic use, and the state's conservative political climate has made it difficult to pass cannabis reform legislation.

However, North Carolina's hemp industry and CBD market offer significant opportunities for growth, particularly in areas like hemp cultivation, product development, and wellness tourism. As demand for hemp-derived products continues to grow, North Carolina's agricultural sector is well-positioned to become a leader in the national hemp industry.

The Future of Cannabis in North Carolina

The future of cannabis in North Carolina will depend on continued advocacy efforts and changes in public opinion. As more North Carolinians become aware of the therapeutic benefits of cannabis, there is hope that the state will eventually adopt a medical cannabis program that allows patients to access cannabis for a broader range of conditions.

The state's growing hemp industry and CBD market will continue to play an important role in shaping the future of cannabis in North Carolina. With its strong agricultural base and commitment to natural health remedies, North Carolina has the potential to become a key player in the national hemp and CBD markets.

If North Carolina eventually legalizes medical or recreational cannabis, the state could unlock new economic opportunities, create jobs, and provide greater access to cannabis for residents across the state. As more states across the U.S. move toward legalization, North Carolina will likely face increasing pressure to join the movement and expand access to cannabis for both medical and recreational use.

Chapter 19: Alabama - A Conservative State's Steps Toward Medical Cannabis

Alabama, a deeply conservative state, has historically resisted cannabis reform. However, in recent years, the state has made notable strides toward establishing a limited medical cannabis program. The passage of the Darren Wesley 'Ato' Hall Compassion Act in 2021 marked a significant turning point for Alabama, creating a framework for the legal use of medical cannabis to treat certain debilitating conditions. While Alabama's cannabis laws remain among the most restrictive in the U.S., the establishment of a medical cannabis program has given advocates hope that the state is slowly moving toward broader reform.

Despite its conservative reputation, Alabama's medical cannabis law reflects a growing recognition of the therapeutic benefits of cannabis for patients with conditions such as chronic pain, epilepsy, and PTSD. Cities like Birmingham, Montgomery, and Mobile are home to communities of patients and advocates who continue to push for broader access to medical cannabis, with the hope that recreational legalization could eventually follow.

The Darren Wesley 'Ato' Hall Compassion Act: Legalizing Medical Cannabis in Alabama

The passage of the Darren Wesley 'Ato' Hall Compassion Act in 2021 marked the beginning of Alabama's journey toward medical cannabis legalization. Named in honor of a young man who suffered from epilepsy and passed away in 2014, the law allows patients with qualifying conditions to legally access medical cannabis products. This historic legislation represented a significant victory for patients and advocates who had long fought for access to cannabis in a state known for its stringent drug laws.

Under the Compassion Act, patients with certain conditions, including epilepsy, cancer, chronic pain, HIV/AIDS, Parkinson's disease, and PTSD, can apply for a medical cannabis card. Once approved, patients will be able to purchase cannabis products from state-licensed dispensaries. However, Alabama's medical cannabis law is highly restrictive, with limitations on the types of products available. Only non-smokable forms of cannabis, such as capsules, gummies, lozenges, and topicals, are permitted under the law.

The Alabama Medical Cannabis Commission (AMCC) is responsible for overseeing the state's medical cannabis program, including the licensing of dispensaries, cultivators, and processors. The commission is tasked with ensuring that cannabis products meet strict safety and quality standards, as well as regulating the distribution of medical cannabis to patients. While the program is still in its early stages, the creation of a legal framework for medical cannabis represents a significant step forward for the state.

Cannabis Advocacy in Alabama

Alabama's cannabis reform efforts have been largely driven by patients and advocates who recognize the therapeutic benefits of medical cannabis. Organizations like Alabama NORML (National Organization for the Reform of Marijuana Laws) and the Alabama Cannabis Industry Association have been at the forefront of efforts to educate lawmakers and the public about the potential benefits of medical cannabis.

Advocates in Alabama have long pushed for a comprehensive medical cannabis program, arguing that patients with debilitating conditions deserve access to safe and effective cannabis treatments. While the state's medical cannabis program remains restrictive, advocates are hopeful that the passage of the Compassion Act will pave the way for future reforms that expand access to a broader range of cannabis products and allow more patients to qualify for the program.

In addition to advocating for medical cannabis, activists in Alabama are also working to reduce the penalties for cannabis possession. Under current Alabama law, possession of even a small amount of cannabis can result in severe criminal penalties, including jail time. Advocates are pushing for the decriminalization of cannabis possession, arguing that the state's harsh penalties disproportionately impact low-income communities and people of color.

Cannabis Culture in Alabama's Major Cities

While Alabama's cannabis laws remain restrictive, the state's cannabis culture is slowly emerging, particularly in cities like Birmingham, Montgomery, and Mobile, where patients and advocates are working to expand access to medical cannabis and raise awareness about its therapeutic benefits.

Birmingham, the largest city in Alabama, has become a hub for cannabis advocacy and patient care. The city is home to a growing community of CBD retailers and wellness centers that offer hemp-derived products to consumers seeking relief from conditions like anxiety, pain, and inflammation. Birmingham's progressive attitude toward cannabis has made it a focal point for efforts to expand the state's medical cannabis program and push for broader cannabis reform.

Montgomery, the state capital, has also seen growing support for medical cannabis, particularly among residents who suffer from chronic conditions and are seeking alternative treatments. While dispensaries have yet to open in Montgomery, the city's residents are increasingly turning to CBD products for relief, and local advocates continue to push for broader access to medical cannabis.

In Mobile, a historic port city on Alabama's Gulf Coast, cannabis culture is slowly gaining traction as more residents become aware of the potential benefits of medical cannabis. Mobile is home to a number of CBD shops and wellness businesses that offer hemp-based products, and the city's residents are actively participating in efforts to expand the state's cannabis program.

Challenges and Opportunities in Alabama's Cannabis Market

Alabama's medical cannabis program is still in its early stages, and the state faces several challenges, particularly in terms of regulatory compliance and market access. The state's restrictive medical cannabis law limits the types of cannabis products that are available to patients, and the lack of smokable flower or full-spectrum cannabis products prevents many patients from accessing the most effective forms of cannabis for their conditions.

Additionally, Alabama's conservative political climate presents significant obstacles to broader cannabis reform, as many state lawmakers remain opposed to the legalization of recreational cannabis. However, growing public support for medical cannabis and the success of programs in other conservative states suggest that further reforms could be possible in the future.

Despite these challenges, Alabama's medical cannabis industry offers significant opportunities for growth, particularly in areas such as patient care, product development, and compliance. As more patients enroll in the state's medical cannabis program, demand for high-quality cannabis products will increase, creating opportunities for dispensaries, cultivators, and processors to thrive.

The Future of Cannabis in Alabama

The future of cannabis in Alabama is full of potential, but progress will likely be gradual. The success of the state's medical cannabis program will depend on continued advocacy efforts and the willingness of lawmakers to expand access to cannabis products for patients in need. As more patients begin using medical cannabis to manage their conditions, public support for cannabis reform is expected to grow, potentially leading to further changes in state law.

Looking ahead, Alabama's hemp industry and CBD market will continue to play an important role in shaping the future of cannabis in the state. With its strong agricultural base and growing demand for hemp-derived products, Alabama is well-positioned to become a leader in the hemp and CBD markets.

If Alabama eventually legalizes recreational cannabis, the state could unlock new economic opportunities, create jobs, and provide greater access to cannabis for residents across the state. As more conservative states in the U.S. move toward cannabis reform, Alabama may follow suit, expanding access to both medical and recreational cannabis.

Chapter 20: Louisiana - The Bayou State's Unique Approach to Cannabis Reform

Louisiana, known for its vibrant culture and rich history, has taken a unique approach to cannabis reform in recent years. While the state has been slower than many others to embrace full cannabis legalization, it has made significant strides in establishing a regulated medical cannabis program. With the passage of several key pieces of legislation over the past decade, Louisiana has laid the foundation for a legal cannabis industry that provides relief to patients while maintaining a strict regulatory framework.

Although recreational cannabis remains illegal in Louisiana, the state's medical marijuana program continues to expand, offering patients access to a wide range of cannabis products. Cities like New Orleans, Baton Rouge, and Lafayette are at the forefront of Louisiana's evolving cannabis culture, with dispensaries, wellness centers, and CBD retailers providing patients and consumers with the tools they need to manage their health and well-being.

Louisiana's Medical Marijuana Program

Louisiana's journey toward cannabis reform began in 2015 with the passage of Act 261, which established the state's medical marijuana program. This law allowed patients with certain debilitating conditions to access medical marijuana, though the program was initially limited in scope. Over the years, Louisiana's medical marijuana program has been expanded through additional legislation, including the passage of Act 96 in 2016, which further broadened the range of qualifying conditions and allowed for the production and distribution of medical cannabis products within the state.

Today, Louisiana's medical marijuana program covers a wide range of qualifying conditions, including cancer, epilepsy, chronic pain, multiple sclerosis, PTSD, and more. Patients must obtain a recommendation from a licensed physician to enroll in the program, after which they can purchase cannabis products from state-licensed dispensaries.

Unlike many other states with medical cannabis programs, Louisiana prohibits the sale of smokable flower. Instead, patients can access tinctures, edibles, topicals, vape cartridges, and capsules.. While this restriction limits the types of products available to patients, Louisiana's medical cannabis industry continues to grow, with increasing demand for high-quality products that provide relief from a variety of medical conditions.

The Role of the Louisiana State University (LSU) and Southern University in Cannabis Production

One of the unique aspects of Louisiana's medical cannabis program is the involvement of the state's two major agricultural universities: Louisiana State University (LSU) and Southern University. These universities are responsible for overseeing the cultivation and production of medical cannabis in the state, in partnership with private companies. LSU's Agricultural Center and Southern University's Agricultural Research and Extension Center have both been granted licenses to produce medical cannabis, ensuring that the products available to patients are of the highest quality and meet stringent regulatory standards.

This partnership between Louisiana's universities and the state's medical cannabis industry reflects a commitment to ensuring that patients have access to safe, effective cannabis products while maintaining strict oversight of the industry. By involving institutions with expertise in agriculture and science, Louisiana has positioned itself as a leader in the research and development of medical cannabis products.

The Dispensary Scene in Louisiana

Louisiana's medical marijuana program is still relatively new, but the state's dispensary scene has grown steadily in recent years. Dispensaries, also known as pharmacies under Louisiana law, are located in cities like New Orleans, Baton Rouge, Lafayette, and Shreveport, providing patients with access to a variety of medical cannabis products.

New Orleans, known for its vibrant culture and progressive attitude, has become a hub for cannabis patients and advocates. Dispensaries in the city offer a range of medical cannabis products, including tinctures, edibles, and vape cartridges, catering to patients with qualifying conditions. New Orleans' rich cultural history, combined with its forward-thinking approach to cannabis reform, makes the city a focal point for Louisiana's growing cannabis industry.

Baton Rouge, the state capital, is home to several licensed dispensaries that serve the needs of medical cannabis patients. Dispensaries in Baton Rouge often focus on patient education, providing resources on the safe use of cannabis and its potential benefits for managing chronic conditions. As the state's political center, Baton Rouge plays an important role in shaping cannabis policy, and advocates continue to push for broader access to cannabis products for patients in need.

In Lafayette, dispensaries provide patients with access to high-quality medical cannabis products, often focusing on the therapeutic benefits of cannabis for conditions like chronic pain, anxiety, and PTSD. Lafayette's growing cannabis community reflects the broader shift toward acceptance of medical cannabis in Louisiana, as more residents turn to cannabis as a natural alternative to traditional pharmaceuticals.

Cannabis Culture in Louisiana's Major Cities

Louisiana's cannabis culture is deeply intertwined with the state's unique identity, combining elements of wellness, community, and natural remedies with the state's rich cultural heritage. In cities like New Orleans, Baton Rouge, and Lafayette, cannabis has become a part of the broader conversation about health and well-being, with dispensaries, wellness centers, and CBD retailers playing a central role in promoting the therapeutic benefits of cannabis.

New Orleans, famous for its Mardi Gras celebrations, music scene, and culinary traditions, has embraced cannabis as part of its progressive culture. Dispensaries in New Orleans often focus on providing high-quality cannabis products that cater to patients seeking relief from a variety of medical conditions. The city's cannabis culture is also reflected in its emphasis on community engagement, with many local businesses and advocates working together to promote cannabis reform and expand access to medical marijuana.

In Baton Rouge, the state's political center, cannabis culture is evolving as more residents advocate for broader access to medical cannabis. Dispensaries in Baton Rouge play a key role in educating patients about the potential benefits of cannabis, while local advocacy groups continue to push for further reforms, including the legalization of recreational cannabis.

Lafayette, a city known for its Cajun culture and food traditions, is home to a growing community of cannabis patients and advocates. The city's dispensaries provide access to medical cannabis products for patients seeking relief from conditions like chronic pain and anxiety, and local businesses are increasingly incorporating CBD products into their offerings.

Cannabis Tourism in Louisiana

Louisiana's vibrant culture and thriving tourism industry make it a prime destination for cannabis tourism, even though recreational cannabis remains illegal. Tourists visiting cities like New Orleans can explore the state's emerging cannabis culture through medical cannabis dispensaries, CBD shops, and wellness centers that offer a range of hemp-derived products.

New Orleans, in particular, is a popular destination for cannabis tourists, thanks to its progressive attitude and reputation as a cultural hub. Visitors can enjoy CBD-infused spa treatments, hemp-friendly yoga classes, and cannabis-themed events while taking in the city's famous jazz music, French Quarter architecture, and culinary delights.

In addition to its urban attractions, Louisiana is home to a growing hemp farming industry, which offers potential opportunities for hemp farm tours and educational experiences that teach visitors about the cultivation and processing of hemp for CBD products and other uses. As Louisiana's hemp industry continues to grow, these types of experiences are likely to become more common, providing tourists with an inside look at the state's emerging cannabis and hemp markets.

Cannabis Festivals and Events in Louisiana

Louisiana's cannabis festivals and hemp expos are gaining popularity as more residents and tourists become interested in the state's growing cannabis market. One of the most well-known events is the Louisiana Hemp Festival, which takes place annually in New Orleans and brings together hemp farmers, cannabis advocates, and industry professionals for a weekend of education, networking, and celebration.

Another major event is the Southern Cannabis Expo, which focuses on the future of the hemp and cannabis industries in Louisiana and the broader Southern U.S. The expo features educational panels, product showcases, and workshops on the latest trends and developments in the cannabis market, making it a valuable resource for anyone involved in the industry.

Challenges and Opportunities in Louisiana's Cannabis Market

Louisiana's cannabis market faces several challenges, particularly in terms of product restrictions and regulatory compliance. The state's medical marijuana program is limited to non-smokable forms of cannabis, which restricts the range of products available to patients. Additionally, the state's regulatory framework is highly complex, making it difficult for businesses to navigate the licensing process and maintain compliance with state laws.

Despite these challenges, Louisiana's cannabis industry offers significant opportunities for growth, particularly in areas such as patient care, research, and CBD product development. As more patients enroll in the state's medical marijuana program, demand for high-quality cannabis products will increase, creating opportunities for dispensaries, cultivators, and processors to thrive.

The Future of Cannabis in Louisiana

The future of cannabis in Louisiana is promising, but progress will likely be gradual. As the state's medical marijuana program continues to expand, advocates will push for further reforms, including the legalization of smokable flower and the creation of a broader range of cannabis products. Additionally, as public support for cannabis reform grows, there is hope that Louisiana will eventually legalize recreational cannabis, creating new economic opportunities and providing greater access to cannabis for residents across the state.

Chapter 21: Mississippi - A Changing Tide for Cannabis Reform

Mississippi, traditionally a conservative state, has recently experienced a shift in public opinion and policy regarding cannabis reform. After years of strict cannabis laws and limited access to medical marijuana, the state made significant progress in 2020 with the passage of Initiative 65, which established a medical cannabis program in Mississippi. Despite some setbacks in implementing the program, the move toward medical cannabis represents a turning point for a state long known for its tough stance on drugs.

Mississippi's cannabis reform is gaining momentum as residents recognize the therapeutic benefits of medical cannabis and push for broader access. Cities like Jackson, Gulfport, and Hattiesburg are leading the charge, with dispensaries, wellness centers, and CBD shops emerging across the state. While recreational cannabis remains illegal, the successful implementation of a medical cannabis program could pave the way for future reforms.

Initiative 65: The Passage of Medical Cannabis in Mississippi

In November 2020, Mississippi voters approved Initiative 65, a citizen-led ballot measure that created a medical cannabis program for patients with debilitating conditions. The passage of Initiative 65 marked a significant victory for patients and advocates who had long fought for access to medical cannabis. The initiative allowed patients with qualifying conditions, such as cancer, epilepsy, chronic pain, PTSD, and multiple sclerosis, to access medical cannabis with a recommendation from a licensed physician.

Under Initiative 65, the Mississippi Department of Health is responsible for regulating the state's medical cannabis program, including issuing licenses to dispensaries, cultivators, and processors. The law allows patients to purchase medical cannabis products from licensed dispensaries, which include flower, edibles, tinctures, and topicals. While smokable flower is permitted under the law, the state imposes strict limits on the amount of cannabis patients can possess at any given time.

Despite the overwhelming support for Initiative 65, the implementation of Mississippi's medical cannabis program faced legal challenges. In May 2021, the Mississippi Supreme Court struck down Initiative 65, citing issues with the state's initiative process. However, in response to the ruling, state lawmakers quickly passed legislation that established a new medical cannabis program, ensuring that patients in Mississippi would still have access to cannabis products.

The Dispensary Scene in Mississippi

Mississippi's dispensary scene is still in its early stages, with licensed dispensaries expected to open in the coming years as the state's medical cannabis program takes shape. These dispensaries will provide patients with access to a variety of cannabis products, including flower, edibles, concentrates, and tinctures, helping patients manage their medical conditions.

Cities like Jackson, Gulfport, and Hattiesburg are expected to become hubs for Mississippi's medical cannabis industry. Jackson, the state capital, is home to a growing community of cannabis advocates and patients, with dispensaries and wellness centers preparing to meet the demand for medical cannabis products. Gulfport, located on the Gulf Coast, is another key city where patients will have access to medical cannabis dispensaries, offering relief for those with qualifying conditions.

In addition to medical cannabis dispensaries, Mississippi is home to a growing number of CBD retailers, which offer a wide range of hemp-derived products that are legal under federal law. These products include CBD tinctures, edibles, and topicals, and they have become popular among residents seeking natural remedies for pain, anxiety, and inflammation.

Cannabis Culture in Mississippi's Major Cities

While Mississippi's cannabis laws remain restrictive, the state's cannabis culture is slowly emerging, particularly in cities like Jackson, Gulfport, and Hattiesburg, where patients and advocates are working to expand access to medical cannabis and raise awareness about its therapeutic benefits.

Jackson, the largest city and capital of Mississippi, has become a focal point for cannabis advocacy and patient care. The city's residents have been at the forefront of efforts to implement the state's medical cannabis program, and Jackson's growing community of CBD retailers and wellness businesses reflects the state's evolving attitudes toward cannabis. As dispensaries begin to open in Jackson, the city is expected to play a key role in shaping the future of cannabis reform in Mississippi.

Gulfport, located along the Gulf of Mexico, has also embraced the potential of medical cannabis. As the second-largest city in Mississippi, Gulfport's residents are increasingly turning to CBD products and are eagerly anticipating the opening of medical cannabis dispensaries. Gulfport's cannabis culture is closely tied to the city's focus on natural health remedies and wellness, with local businesses offering products and services designed to promote relaxation and holistic healing.

In Hattiesburg, a college town known for its vibrant community and progressive attitudes, cannabis culture is steadily growing. Hattiesburg, home to the University of Southern Mississippi, has become a key location for the state's evolving cannabis scene, particularly as younger residents advocate for cannabis reform and embrace the therapeutic benefits of CBD and medical cannabis. With the potential opening of medical cannabis dispensaries, Hattiesburg's cannabis culture is expected to continue flourishing, contributing to the broader movement for cannabis legalization in Mississippi.

Cannabis Tourism in Mississippi

While recreational cannabis remains illegal in Mississippi, the state's CBD industry and emerging medical cannabis market are beginning to attract visitors interested in wellness tourism and natural remedies. Cities like Jackson and Gulfport offer tourists access to a growing number of CBD shops, wellness centers, and hemp farms, providing a unique way for visitors to experience Mississippi's evolving cannabis culture.

Jackson, as the state capital, is likely to become a hub for medical cannabis patients and cannabis tourists, particularly as dispensaries begin to open and the state's medical cannabis program gains momentum. Tourists visiting Jackson can explore the city's rich history and cultural attractions while also learning about the therapeutic uses of cannabis through wellness centers and CBD retailers.

Gulfport, with its scenic coastline and popular tourist destinations, also offers potential for cannabis-friendly tourism as the state's medical cannabis industry develops. Visitors to Gulfport can enjoy CBD-infused spa treatments, hemp-friendly yoga classes, and explore local CBD products while taking in the beauty of the Gulf Coast.

Cannabis Festivals and Events in Mississippi

As Mississippi's cannabis industry continues to grow, the state is seeing a rise in cannabis-themed festivals, expos, and educational events that celebrate the state's emerging cannabis market. One of the most notable events is the Mississippi Cannabis Expo, which brings together patients, advocates, and industry professionals to discuss the latest developments in the medical cannabis industry and explore the future of cannabis in Mississippi.

Another popular event is the Southern Hemp Expo, which takes place in cities across the Southeast, including Mississippi, and focuses on the potential of the hemp industry in the region. The expo features educational panels, product showcases, and networking opportunities for those involved in the CBD and hemp industries.

In addition to these larger events, Mississippi is home to a growing number of CBD-friendly markets, pop-up shops, and wellness retreats that promote the health benefits of hemp-derived products. These events provide consumers with the opportunity to learn more about the therapeutic uses of cannabis and connect with local CBD and medical cannabis businesses.

Challenges and Opportunities in Mississippi's Cannabis Market

Mississippi's cannabis market faces several challenges, particularly in terms of regulatory hurdles and limited access to cannabis products. The legal challenges surrounding Initiative 65, as well as the state's slow rollout of its medical cannabis program, have made it difficult for patients to access medical cannabis products. Additionally, Mississippi's conservative political climate presents obstacles to broader cannabis reform, including the potential legalization of recreational cannabis.

However, despite these challenges, Mississippi's cannabis industry offers significant opportunities for growth, particularly in areas such as patient care, CBD product development, and hemp cultivation. As demand for medical cannabis products continues to grow, there is potential for dispensaries, cultivators, and processors to thrive in the state's emerging market. Mississippi's strong agricultural base also positions the state as a leader in hemp production, creating opportunities for farmers and entrepreneurs in the CBD market.

The Future of Cannabis in Mississippi

The future of cannabis in Mississippi is full of potential, with the state's medical cannabis program set to expand in the coming years. As dispensaries begin to open and more patients enroll in the program, advocates are hopeful that the state will continue to improve access to medical cannabis and eventually move toward the legalization of recreational cannabis.

As public support for cannabis reform grows, there is increasing pressure on state lawmakers to expand the medical cannabis program and ensure that patients can access a broader range of cannabis products. Additionally, the state's growing hemp industry and CBD market will continue to play an important role in shaping the future of cannabis in Mississippi.

Looking ahead, Mississippi has the potential to become a major player in the Southern cannabis market, particularly as other states in the region, such as Louisiana and Alabama, also move toward cannabis reform. If Mississippi fully embraces cannabis legalization, the state could unlock new economic opportunities, create jobs, and provide greater access to cannabis for residents across the state.

Chapter 22: Tennessee - A Conservative State Slowly Embracing Cannabis Reform

Tennessee, known for its rich musical heritage and conservative political landscape, has been slow to embrace cannabis reform compared to other states. Despite its resistance to legalizing recreational cannabis or establishing a full medical marijuana program, the state has taken small steps toward reform, particularly in the areas of CBD and hemp cultivation. The 2018 Farm Bill, which legalized the production of hemp across the United States, has played a significant role in shaping Tennessee's emerging cannabis market, allowing the state's farmers and entrepreneurs to explore opportunities in CBD production and hemp-derived products.

While Tennessee has yet to legalize medical marijuana, the state has a thriving CBD industry that caters to residents seeking natural remedies for conditions like anxiety, pain, and insomnia. Cities like Nashville, Memphis, and Knoxville are leading the way in Tennessee's evolving cannabis culture, with CBD shops, wellness centers, and hemp farms driving demand for hemp-derived products. Advocates continue to push for broader cannabis reform, particularly for the legalization of medical marijuana, as more Tennesseans recognize the therapeutic benefits of cannabis.

The Role of CBD and Hemp in Tennessee's Cannabis Market

Tennessee's cannabis industry is centered around CBD and hemp-derived products, which are legal under the 2018 Farm Bill as long as they contain less than 0.3% THC. The state's hemp industry has grown rapidly since the passage of the Farm Bill, with Tennessee farmers embracing the opportunity to cultivate hemp for CBD extraction and other industrial applications. The state's favorable climate for hemp cultivation, combined with its agricultural heritage, has positioned Tennessee as a leading producer of hemp in the Southeastern United States.

The success of the CBD market in Tennessee has normalized cannabis use for many residents, even as the state maintains its strict stance on marijuana. CBD products, including tinctures, edibles, topicals, and vape cartridges, are widely available across the state and have become popular among consumers seeking relief from conditions like chronic pain, anxiety, and sleep disorders. Many Tennesseans have turned to CBD as a natural alternative to prescription medications, further fueling demand for hemp-derived products.

In addition to the state's growing hemp industry, Tennessee has established a legal framework for the production and sale of CBD products, creating opportunities for entrepreneurs to launch CBD brands, open CBD shops, and participate in the state's hemp economy. Cities like Nashville and Memphis have embraced CBD culture, with numerous businesses catering to consumers interested in the therapeutic benefits of cannabis.

Cannabis Advocacy in Tennessee

Despite Tennessee's conservative stance on cannabis, there is a growing movement among residents and advocates to push for broader cannabis reform, particularly the legalization of medical marijuana. Organizations like Tennessee NORML (National Organization for the Reform of Marijuana Laws) and Safe Access Tennessee have been at the forefront of efforts to educate lawmakers and the public about the benefits of medical cannabis and to advocate for a comprehensive medical marijuana program.

Advocates argue that patients with debilitating conditions, such as chronic pain, epilepsy, PTSD, and cancer, deserve access to medical cannabis as a safe and effective treatment option. Currently, Tennessee allows limited access to low-THC CBD oil for patients with seizure disorders, but the state has not yet established a full medical marijuana program. Advocates continue to push for legislation that would expand access to medical cannabis for a wider range of conditions, allowing more patients to benefit from the therapeutic properties of cannabis.

In addition to advocating for medical cannabis, activists in Tennessee are also working to decriminalize cannabis possession. Under current Tennessee law, possession of even small amounts of cannabis is a criminal offense that can result in severe penalties, including jail time. Advocacy groups are pushing for decriminalization measures that would reduce the penalties for cannabis possession, making it easier for individuals to avoid criminal charges for minor offenses.

Cannabis Culture in Tennessee's Major Cities

While Tennessee's cannabis laws remain restrictive, the state's cannabis culture is emerging in cities like Nashville, Memphis, and Knoxville, where CBD products are widely available and residents are increasingly advocating for cannabis reform. These cities are home to thriving CBD markets, with CBD shops, hemp farms, and wellness centers contributing to the state's evolving cannabis scene.

Nashville, known as Music City, has become a hub for cannabis advocates and entrepreneurs. The city's progressive attitude and focus on wellness have made it a focal point for the state's CBD industry, with numerous CBD retailers offering a wide range of products, from CBD-infused beverages to CBD skin care products. Nashville's residents are at the forefront of efforts to push for medical cannabis legalization, and the city's CBD culture is closely tied to its emphasis on health, creativity, and natural remedies.

Memphis, located along the Mississippi River, is another key city in Tennessee's cannabis landscape. The city's CBD shops and hemp farms have become popular destinations for residents seeking relief from a variety of health conditions, and Memphis' strong sense of community has helped foster a supportive environment for cannabis reform. Advocates in Memphis are actively working to expand access to medical cannabis, with many residents expressing frustration over the state's slow progress on cannabis legislation.

Knoxville, a college town home to the University of Tennessee, has also seen growing support for cannabis reform. The city's residents are increasingly turning to CBD products as a natural alternative to traditional medicine, and Knoxville's focus on wellness and natural health remedies has helped shape the city's emerging cannabis culture. As more residents advocate for medical cannabis, Knoxville is expected to play an important role in pushing for broader cannabis reform in Tennessee.

Cannabis Tourism in Tennessee

While recreational cannabis remains illegal in Tennessee, the state's CBD market and hemp industry are attracting tourists interested in wellness tourism and natural remedies. Visitors to cities lik Nashville and Memphis can explore the state's growing CBD industry, visiting CBD shops, hemp farms, and wellness centers that offer a variety of hemp-derived product.

Nashville is a popular destination for tourists seeking CBD-friendly experiences, with many local businesses offering CBD-infused beverages, CBD massages, and hemp-based skincare products. Visitors to Nashville can enjoy the city's vibrant music scene while exploring its cannabis culture, which is centered around the therapeutic benefits of hemp-derived products.

Memphis, with its rich musical history and cultural significance, is also a destination for tourists interested in CBD tourism. The city's growing number of CBD retailers and hemp farms provide visitors with a unique way to experience Tennessee's cannabis culture, while also enjoying the city's famous barbecue and blues music.

Cannabis Festivals and Events in Tennessee

As Tennessee's cannabis industry continues to develop, the state is seeing a rise in hemp and CBD-themed festivals, expos, and educational events that celebrate the state's evolving cannabis market. One of the most notable events is the Tennessee Hemp Expo, which brings together farmers, entrepreneurs, and advocates to discuss the latest developments in the hemp and CBD industries.

Another popular event is the Southern Hemp Expo, which focuses on the future of hemp and CBD in Tennessee and the broader Southern United States. The expo features educational panels, product showcases, and networking opportunities for those involved in the CBD and hemp markets.

In addition to these larger events, Tennessee is home to a growing number of CBD-friendly pop-up shops, markets, and wellness retreats that promote the health benefits of hemp-derived products. These events provide consumers with an opportunity to learn more about the therapeutic uses of cannabis and connect with local CBD businesses.

Challenges and Opportunities in Tennessee's Cannabis Market

Tennessee's cannabis market faces several challenges, particularly in terms of regulatory hurdles and the lack of a medical cannabis program. While the state's CBD industry has flourished, the absence of a comprehensive medical marijuana program has left many patients without access to cannabis products that could improve their quality of life. Additionally, Tennessee's conservative political climate presents obstacles to broader cannabis reform, as many lawmakers remain opposed to cannabis legalization.

The Future of Cannabis in Tennessee

The future of cannabis in Tennessee will depend on continued advocacy efforts and changes in public opinion. As more Tennesseans become aware of the therapeutic benefits of cannabis, there is hope that the state will eventually adopt a medical cannabis program that allows patients to access cannabis for a broader range of conditions.

The state's growing hemp industry and CBD market will continue to play an important role in shaping the future of cannabis in Tennessee. With its strong agricultural base and growing demand for CBD products, Tennessee has the potential to become a leader in the national hemp and CBD markets. As more Tennesseans turn to CBD and hemp-derived products for their health and wellness needs, public support for cannabis reform is expected to increase.

Advocates for medical cannabis continue to push for legislation that would establish a comprehensive medical marijuana program in Tennessee. If the state adopts such a program, it could significantly improve access to cannabis-based therapies for patients with conditions like chronic pain, PTSD, and epilepsy, allowing more residents to benefit from the therapeutic properties of cannabis.

Looking ahead, Tennessee may eventually consider the legalization of recreational cannabis, particularly as neighboring states move toward cannabis reform. If Tennessee fully embraces cannabis legalization, the state could unlock new economic opportunities, create jobs, and provide greater access to cannabis for residents across the state.

As the broader conversation around cannabis reform continues to evolve, Tennessee will likely face increasing pressure from both residents and neighboring states to expand access to medical and recreational cannabis. The future of cannabis in Tennessee remains uncertain, but with continued advocacy and growing public support, the state may ultimately join the movement toward cannabis legalization in the U.S.

Chapter 23: Kentucky - The Role of Hemp in Shaping Cannabis Reform

Kentucky has a long and storied history with hemp cultivation, dating back to the 18th century when the state was a leading producer of hemp in the United States. As one of the few states where hemp cultivation remained a significant agricultural industry, Kentucky's relationship with the hemp plant is central to its evolving stance on cannabis reform. While the state has yet to legalize recreational cannabis or establish a full medical marijuana program, Kentucky has embraced hemp production and CBD as key drivers of its cannabis industry.

The 2014 and 2018 federal Farm Bills have played pivotal roles in reestablishing Kentucky as a leader in hemp production. Today, the state's thriving hemp industry and growing CBD market are helping to shift public opinion on cannabis reform, particularly as more residents recognize the therapeutic benefits of cannabis-derived products. Cities like Lexington, Louisville, and Bowling Green are at the forefront of Kentucky's cannabis culture, with hemp farms, CBD shops, and wellness centers contributing to the state's evolving approach to cannabis.

Kentucky's History with Hemp Cultivation

Kentucky has a long history of hemp production, dating back to the 1700s when farmers in the state began cultivating hemp for use in textiles, ropes, and sails. By the 19th century, Kentucky was the leading producer of hemp in the United States, with thousands of acres dedicated to hemp cultivation. The state's rich soil and favorable climate made it an ideal location for hemp farming, and Kentucky's agricultural industry thrived as a result.

However, the Marihuana Tax Act of 1937 and subsequent federal regulations on cannabis led to a decline in hemp production across the United States, including in Kentucky. The War on Drugs further stigmatized the plant, and hemp production was banned in the U.S. in 1970 under the Controlled Substances Act, which classified hemp as a Schedule I drug alongside marijuana.

In recent years, the passage of the 2014 and 2018 Farm Bills has allowed for the reintroduction of industrial hemp cultivation in Kentucky and other states. Kentucky has embraced its hemp heritage, reemerging as a leader in hemp production and CBD extraction, with farmers and entrepreneurs capitalizing on the growing demand for hemp-derived products.

The Role of Hemp in Kentucky's Cannabis Market

Kentucky's modern cannabis industry is centered around the hemp plant and CBD products, both of which are legal under federal law as long as they contain less than 0.3% THC. The state's hemp industry has experienced rapid growth since the passage of the 2018 Farm Bill, with Kentucky farmers producing hemp for CBD extraction, fiber, and grain. The state's fertile land and agricultural expertise make it one of the leading hemp producers in the United States.

The success of the CBD market in Kentucky has helped normalize cannabis use for many residents, even as the state maintains its strict stance on marijuana. CBD products, including tinctures, edibles, topicals, and vape products, are widely available across Kentucky and have become popular among consumers seeking natural remedies for conditions like chronic pain, anxiety, and sleep disorders.

In addition to the state's hemp farms, Kentucky has established a robust legal framework for CBD production, creating opportunities for entrepreneurs to launch CBD brands, open CBD shops, and participate in the state's hemp economy. Cities like Lexington and Louisville have embraced the CBD industry, with numerous businesses catering to consumers interested in the therapeutic benefits of hemp-derived products.

Cannabis Advocacy in Kentucky

Despite Kentucky's conservative stance on marijuana legalization, there is a growing movement among residents and advocates to push for broader cannabis reform, particularly the legalization of medical marijuana. Advocacy groups like Kentucky NORML (National Organization for the Reform of Marijuana Laws) and Kentucky for Medical Marijuana have been at the forefront of efforts to educate lawmakers and the public about the benefits of medical cannabis and to push for the creation of a comprehensive medical marijuana program in the state.

Advocates argue that patients with debilitating conditions, such as chronic pain, epilepsy, PTSD, and cancer, should have access to medical cannabis as a safe and effective treatment option. Kentucky has yet to pass legislation that would establish a full medical marijuana program, but recent efforts by state lawmakers have indicated a growing interest in exploring cannabis reform.

In addition to advocating for medical cannabis, activists in Kentucky are working to decriminalize cannabis possession. Under current state law, possession of even small amounts of cannabis is a criminal offense that can result in severe penalties, including jail time. Advocacy groups are pushing for decriminalization measures that would reduce the penalties for cannabis possession, particularly for nonviolent offenses.

Cannabis Culture in Kentucky's Major Cities

While Kentucky's cannabis laws remain restrictive, the state's cannabis culture is emerging in cities like Lexington, Louisville, and Bowling Green, where CBD products are widely available and residents are increasingly advocating for cannabis reform. These cities are home to thriving CBD markets, with CBD shops, hemp farms, and wellness centers contributing to the state's evolving cannabis scene.

Lexington, known for its horse farms and agricultural heritage, has become a hub for cannabis advocates and entrepreneurs. The city's CBD shops and hemp farms offer a wide range of hemp-derived products, including CBD-infused beverages, topicals, and edibles, catering to consumers seeking natural remedies for health and wellness. Lexington's residents are at the forefront of efforts to push for medical cannabis legalization, and the city's CBD culture is closely tied to its emphasis on health and agriculture.

Louisville, Kentucky's largest city, is another key player in the state's cannabis landscape. The city's CBD retailers and hemp businesses have become popular destinations for residents seeking relief from a variety of health conditions, and Louisville's strong sense of community has helped foster a supportive environment for cannabis reform. Local businesses are increasingly incorporating CBD into their offerings, and Louisville's residents are actively participating in efforts to expand access to medical cannabis.

In Bowling Green, a college town known for its vibrant community and progressive attitudes, cannabis culture is steadily growing. The city's CBD shops and wellness centers provide residents with access to hemp-derived products that promote relaxation and natural health remedies. As more residents advocate for medical cannabis, Bowling Green is expected to play an important role in pushing for broader cannabis reform in Kentucky.

Cannabis Tourism in Kentucky

While recreational cannabis remains illegal in Kentucky, the state's CBD market and hemp industry are attracting visitors interested in wellness tourism and hemp farming. Visitors to cities like Lexington and Louisville can explore the state's growing CBD industry, visiting CBD shops, hemp farms, and wellness centers that offer a variety of hemp-derived products.

Lexington is a popular destination for tourists seeking CBD-friendly experiences, with many local businesses offering CBD-infused beverages, hemp-friendly tours, and hemp-based skincare products. Visitors to Lexington can enjoy the city's agricultural heritage while exploring its hemp culture, which is centered around the therapeutic benefits of hemp-derived products.

In addition to its urban attractions, Kentucky is home to a growing hemp farming industry, which offers potential opportunities for hemp farm tours and educational experiences that teach visitors about the cultivation and processing of hemp for CBD extraction and other industrial applications. As Kentucky's hemp industry continues to grow, these types of experiences are likely to become more common, providing tourists with an inside look at the state's emerging cannabis and hemp markets.

Cannabis Festivals and Events in Kentucky

Kentucky is seeing a rise in hemp and CBD-themed festivals, expos, and educational events that celebrate the state's evolving cannabis market. One of the most notable events is the Kentucky Hemp Festival, which brings together farmers, entrepreneurs, and advocates to discuss the latest developments in the hemp and CBD industries.

Another popular event is the Southern Hemp Expo, which takes place in cities across the Southern U.S., including Kentucky, and focuses on the potential of hemp and CBD in the region. The expo features educational panels, product showcases, and networking opportunities for those involved in the hemp market.

Challenges and Opportunities in Kentucky's Cannabis Market

Kentucky's cannabis market faces several challenges, particularly in terms of regulatory barriers and the lack of a medical cannabis program. While the state's CBD industry has flourished, the absence of a comprehensive medical marijuana program has left many patients without access to cannabis products that could improve their quality of life. Additionally, Kentucky's conservative political climate presents obstacles to broader cannabis reform.

Despite these challenges, Kentucky's hemp industry offers significant opportunities for growth, particularly in areas like hemp cultivation, product development, and wellness tourism. As demand for CBD products continues to grow, Kentucky is well-positioned to become a leader in the national hemp and CBD markets, creating opportunities for farmers, entrepreneurs, and retailers. Kentucky's strong agricultural base and favorable climate for hemp cultivation make it an ideal location for the expansion of the hemp industry, and the state's growing demand for CBD products reflects a shift in public opinion toward the therapeutic benefits of cannabis-derived products.

The Future of Cannabis in Kentucky

The future of cannabis in Kentucky will depend largely on continued advocacy efforts and changes in public opinion. As more Kentuckians become aware of the health benefits of cannabis, there is growing support for the establishment of a comprehensive medical marijuana program. Advocates are hopeful that state lawmakers will recognize the need for cannabis reform and pass legislation that allows patients to access medical cannabis for a wider range of conditions.

The state's growing hemp industry and CBD market will continue to play an important role in shaping the future of cannabis in Kentucky. With its rich agricultural history and favorable conditions for hemp farming, Kentucky is well-positioned to capitalize on the booming hemp market, offering opportunities for local businesses and farmers to thrive.

Looking ahead, Kentucky may eventually consider the legalization of recreational cannabis, particularly as neighboring states move toward cannabis reform. If Kentucky fully embraces cannabis legalization, the state could unlock new economic opportunities, create jobs, and provide greater access to cannabis for residents across the state. As more states across the U.S. move toward legalization, Kentucky will likely face increasing pressure to join the movement and expand access to medical and recreational cannabis.

Chapter 24: Indiana - Navigating Cannabis Reform in the Heartland

Indiana, located in the heartland of the United States, is known for its conservative stance on cannabis. Despite the progress made by neighboring states in cannabis reform, Indiana has remained one of the most restrictive states in terms of marijuana legislation. Both medical marijuana and recreational cannabis remain illegal in Indiana, and the state enforces strict penalties for cannabis possession. However, there is growing momentum among residents and advocates for reform, particularly in the area of medical cannabis.

While Indiana has yet to embrace cannabis reform on a large scale, the state has made some progress in legalizing hemp and CBD products. Following the passage of the 2018 Farm Bill, Indiana legalized the cultivation and production of industrial hemp, allowing the state's farmers to explore opportunities in the hemp industry. Indiana also permits the sale of CBD products that contain less than 0.3% THC, and the CBD market has become a thriving industry in the state's cities, including Indianapolis, Fort Wayne, and Bloomington.

The CBD and Hemp Market in Indiana

Indiana's modern cannabis industry is primarily centered around CBD products and hemp cultivation, both of which are legal under federal law as long as they meet the 0.3% THC threshold. The state's hemp industry has grown since the legalization of industrial hemp in 2018, with Indiana farmers embracing the opportunity to cultivate hemp for CBD extraction and other uses. Hemp farming has become an important part of Indiana's agricultural landscape, and many of the state's farmers are capitalizing on the growing demand for hemp-derived products.

The success of the CBD market in Indiana has helped normalize cannabis use for many residents, even as the state maintains its strict stance on marijuana legalization. CBD products, including tinctures, edibles, topicals, and vape products, are widely available across Indiana and have become popular among consumers seeking natural remedies for conditions like chronic pain, anxiety, and sleep disorders.

In addition to the state's growing CBD industry, Indiana has established a legal framework for hemp production, creating opportunities for entrepreneurs to launch CBD brands, open CBD shops, and participate in the state's hemp economy. Cities like Indianapolis and Fort Wayne have embraced the CBD industry, with numerous businesses catering to consumers interested in the therapeutic benefits of hemp-derived products.

Cannabis Advocacy in Indiana

While Indiana remains one of the most restrictive states in terms of cannabis laws, there is a growing movement among residents and advocates to push for cannabis reform, particularly the legalization of medical marijuana. Organizations like Indiana NORML (National Organization for the Reform of Marijuana Laws) and Hoosier Veterans for Medical Cannabis have been at the forefront of efforts to educate lawmakers and the public about the benefits of medical cannabis and to push for the creation of a comprehensive medical marijuana program in the state.

Advocates argue that patients with debilitating conditions, such as chronic pain, PTSD, epilepsy, and cancer, deserve access to medical cannabis as a safe and effective treatment option. Currently, Indiana does not allow for the use of medical marijuana, but advocates continue to push for legislation that would expand access to cannabis for patients in need.

In addition to advocating for medical cannabis, activists in Indiana are working to reduce the penalties for cannabis possession. Under current Indiana law, possession of even small amounts of cannabis is a criminal offense that can result in harsh penalties, including jail time. Advocacy groups are pushing for decriminalization measures that would reduce the penalties for cannabis possession, making it easier for individuals to avoid criminal charges for minor offenses.

Cannabis Culture in Indiana's Major Cities

While Indiana's cannabis laws remain restrictive, the state's cannabis culture is slowly emerging, particularly in cities like Indianapolis, Fort Wayne, and Bloomington, where CBD products are widely available and residents are increasingly advocating for cannabis reform. These cities are home to thriving CBD markets, with CBD shops, hemp farms, and wellness centers contributing to the state's evolving cannabis scene.

Indianapolis, the capital and largest city in Indiana, has become a hub for cannabis advocates and entrepreneurs. The city's progressive attitude and focus on wellness have made it a focal point for the state's CBD industry, with numerous CBD retailers offering a wide range of products, from CBD-infused beverages to CBD skincare products. Indianapolis' residents are at the forefront of efforts to push for medical cannabis legalization, and the city's CBD culture is closely tied to its emphasis on health and wellness.

Fort Wayne, the second-largest city in Indiana, has also embraced the potential of CBD products. The city's CBD shops and wellness centers have become popular destinations for residents seeking relief from a variety of health conditions, and Fort Wayne's community-driven approach to health and wellness has helped foster a supportive environment for cannabis reform.

Bloomington, a college town home to Indiana University, is known for its progressive culture and has been a key player in the state's cannabis advocacy efforts. The city's residents are increasingly turning to CBD products as a natural alternative to traditional medicine, and Bloomington's wellness-focused community has played an important role in pushing for broader cannabis reform in Indiana.

Cannabis Tourism in Indiana

Indianapolis is a popular destination for tourists seeking CBD-friendly experiences, with many local businesses offering CBD-infused products, CBD massages, and hemp-based skincare products. Visitors to Indianapolis can enjoy the city's vibrant culture while exploring its cannabis culture, which is centered around the therapeutic benefits of hemp-derived products.

Bloomington, known for its lively college atmosphere and progressive values, also offers tourists a chance to explore Indiana's emerging CBD market. Visitors to Bloomington can enjoy the city's CBD shops and wellness retreats, which offer a variety of CBD products designed to promote relaxation and holistic health.

Cannabis Festivals and Events in Indiana

Indiana is seeing a rise in hemp and CBD-themed festivals, expos, and educational events that celebrate the state's evolving cannabis market. One of the most notable events is the Indiana Cannabis Awards, which recognizes CBD businesses, hemp farmers, and cannabis advocates for their contributions to the industry.

Another popular event is the Midwest Hemp Expo, which takes place in Indiana and focuses on the future of hemp and CBD in the region. The expo features educational panels, product showcases, and networking opportunities for those involved in the hemp and CBD industries.

In addition to these larger events, Indiana is home to a growing number of CBD-friendly pop-up markets, wellness retreats, and educational workshop that promote the health benefits of hemp-derived products. These events provide consumers with an opportunity to learn more about the therapeutic uses of cannabis and connect with local CBD businesses.

Challenges and Opportunities in Indiana's Cannabis Market

Indiana's cannabis market faces several challenges, particularly in terms of regulatory barriers and the lack of a medical cannabis program. While the state's CBD industry has flourished, the absence of a comprehensive medical marijuana program has left many patients without access to cannabis products that could improve their quality of life. Additionally, Indiana's conservative political climate presents obstacles to broader cannabis reform, as many lawmakers remain opposed to cannabis legalization.

Despite these challenges, Indiana's CBD market and hemp industry offer significant opportunities for growth, particularly in areas like hemp cultivation, CBD product development, and wellness tourism. As demand for CBD products continues to grow, Indiana is well-positioned to become a leader in the national hemp market, creating opportunities for farmers, entrepreneurs, and retailers.

The Future of Cannabis in Indiana

The future of cannabis in Indiana will depend largely on continued advocacy efforts and changes in public opinion. As more Hoosiers become aware of the therapeutic benefits of cannabis, there is growing support for the establishment of a comprehensive medical marijuana program. Advocates are hopeful that state lawmakers will recognize the need for cannabis reform and pass legislation that allows patients to access medical cannabis for a broader range of conditions.

The state's growing hemp industry and CBD market will continue to play an important role in shaping the future of cannabis in Indiana. With its strong agricultural base and favorable conditions for hemp farming, Indiana is well-positioned to capitalize on the booming hemp market, offering opportunities for local businesses and farmers to thrive.

Looking ahead, Indiana may eventually consider the legalization of recreational cannabis, particularly as neighboring states move toward cannabis reform. If Indiana fully embraces cannabis legalization, the state could unlock new economic opportunities, create jobs, and provide greater access to cannabis for residents across the state. As more states across the U.S. move toward cannabis legalization, Indiana will likely face increasing pressure to join the movement and expand access to medical and recreational cannabis.

The ongoing success of Indiana's hemp industry and CBD market suggests that the state has a foundation for future cannabis reforms. As demand for hemp-derived products continues to grow, Indiana may see more residents, business owners, and farmers advocating for broader cannabis policies. The state's agricultural strength, combined with increasing public support for cannabis reform, makes Indiana well-positioned to explore the economic and health benefits of a more comprehensive cannabis industry.

The future of cannabis reform in Indiana depends on continued advocacy, education, and legislative action. If the state eventually legalizes medical cannabis or even recreational cannabis, it could not only improve patient access to therapeutic cannabis products but also create significant economic opportunities for the state.

Chapter 25: Missouri - Medical Marijuana and the Path to Full Legalization

Missouri has made significant strides in cannabis reform over the past few years, particularly with the legalization of medical marijuana in 2018. The state's evolving approach to cannabis, driven by growing public support and advocacy efforts, has led to the development of a robust medical cannabis market that provides patients with access to a wide range of cannabis products. While recreational cannabis remains illegal, Missouri's medical cannabis program is paving the way for broader cannabis reform, and there is increasing discussion around the potential for full adult-use legalization.

Cities like St. Louis, Kansas City, and Columbia are at the forefront of Missouri's emerging cannabis culture, with dispensaries, wellness centers, and cannabis-friendly events contributing to the state's growing market. Missouri's cannabis industry is expanding rapidly, offering new economic opportunities and improving patient access to medical marijuana.

The Passage of Medical Marijuana in Missouri

In 2018, Missouri voters approved Amendment 2, a ballot initiative that legalized medical marijuana in the state. The passage of Amendment 2 marked a major milestone for cannabis reform in Missouri, creating a legal framework for the cultivation, production, and sale of medical cannabis. Under the amendment, patients with qualifying conditions, such as chronic pain, PTSD, epilepsy, and cancer, can apply for a medical marijuana card, allowing them to purchase cannabis products from licensed dispensaries.

Missouri's medical marijuana program is overseen by the Missouri Department of Health and Senior Services (DHSS), which is responsible for issuing licenses to cultivators, processors, dispensaries, and caregivers. Since the program's launch, Missouri has become one of the fastest-growing medical cannabis markets in the United States, with thousands of patients enrolling in the program and dozens of dispensaries opening across the state.

One of the unique aspects of Missouri's medical marijuana program is its patient-friendly policies. Patients are allowed to grow up to six plants for personal use, and the state's medical cannabis card system is designed to provide affordable access to cannabis products for patients in need. Additionally, Missouri's medical marijuana laws include provisions for caregivers, allowing them to assist patients with purchasing and cultivating cannabis.

The Dispensary Scene in Missouri

Missouri's dispensary scene has grown rapidly since the legalization of medical marijuana, with licensed dispensaries opening in cities across the state. St. Louis, Kansas City, and Columbia have become key locations for medical cannabis dispensaries, offering patients access to a wide variety of cannabis products, including flower, edibles, tinctures, concentrates, and topicals.

St. Louis, the largest city in Missouri, has emerged as a hub for the state's medical marijuana industry. The city is home to numerous dispensaries that provide patients with access to high-quality cannabis products for a variety of conditions. St. Louis' growing cannabis culture is closely tied to its emphasis on health and wellness, with local businesses offering educational resources on the therapeutic benefits of cannabis.

Kansas City, located on the western edge of Missouri, is another major player in the state's medical marijuana market. Dispensaries in Kansas City offer a wide range of cannabis products, catering to patients with a diverse set of medical conditions. Kansas City's cannabis community is highly active, with local advocates working to expand access to cannabis for both medical and recreational use.

In Columbia, a college town known for its progressive values, medical cannabis dispensaries have become popular destinations for residents seeking natural health remedies. Columbia's dispensaries provide patients with access to a variety of cannabis-based therapies, helping to foster a growing sense of community around cannabis reform and patient care.

Cannabis Advocacy in Missouri

Missouri's cannabis reform movement has been largely driven by patients, advocates, and organizations dedicated to expanding access to medical cannabis and pushing for the legalization of recreational cannabis. Groups like Missouri NORML (National Organization for the Reform of Marijuana Laws) and New Approach Missouri played a key role in the passage of Amendment 2, and they continue to advocate for broader cannabis reform in the state.

Advocates argue that the success of Missouri's medical marijuana program is evidence that the state is ready for recreational cannabis legalization. As more Missourians become aware of the therapeutic benefits of cannabis, public support for adult-use legalization is growing. Recent polling data suggests that a majority of Missouri residents support the legalization of recreational cannabis, and there is increasing pressure on state lawmakers to pass legislation that would allow adults over the age of 21 to purchase and use cannabis for recreational purposes.

In addition to pushing for recreational legalization, advocates are also working to improve the state's medical marijuana program, particularly in the areas of patient access and affordability. While Missouri's program is one of the most patient-friendly in the country, there are still concerns about the cost of cannabis products and the availability of dispensaries in rural areas. Advocates are calling for reforms that would make medical cannabis more accessible to patients across the state, regardless of their location or income level.

Cannabis Culture in Missouri's Major Cities

Missouri's cannabis culture is rapidly evolving, particularly in cities like St. Louis, Kansas City, and Columbia, where medical marijuana dispensaries and cannabis-friendly events are becoming more common. These cities are home to thriving cannabis communities, with local businesses, advocates, and patients working together to promote the therapeutic benefits of cannabis and push for broader cannabis reform.

St. Louis, known for its rich history and vibrant arts scene, has embraced the medical cannabis industry, with numerous dispensaries and wellness centers catering to patients seeking natural health remedies. The city's cannabis culture is closely tied to its focus on wellness, with many local businesses offering educational resources on the use of medical cannabis for conditions like chronic pain, anxiety, and PTSD.

Kansas City, with its strong sense of community and progressive values, has become a key player in Missouri's cannabis movement. The city's dispensaries provide patients with access to a wide range of cannabis products, and local advocacy groups are working to expand access to both medical and recreational cannabis. Kansas City's cannabis culture is closely aligned with its emphasis on community health and well-being, making it an ideal location for the state's cannabis reform movement.

In Columbia, home to the University of Missouri, cannabis culture is thriving as more residents turn to medical marijuana for relief from a variety of conditions. The city's dispensaries provide patients with access to cannabis-based therapies, and Columbia's progressive attitudes have made it a focal point for efforts to expand access to medical cannabis and push for recreational legalization.

Cannabis Tourism in Missouri

While recreational cannabis is not yet legal in Missouri, the state's medical marijuana program and CBD industry are attracting visitors interested in wellness tourism and natural health remedies. Cities like St. Louis and Kansas City offer tourists access to medical cannabis dispensaries, CBD shops, and cannabis-friendly wellness centers, providing a unique way for visitors to experience Missouri's emerging cannabis culture.

St. Louis, with its vibrant cultural scene and historical significance, is a popular destination for cannabis tourists seeking medical cannabis or CBD-infused products. Visitors to St. Louis can explore the city's numerous dispensaries and wellness centers, which offer a variety of cannabis-based therapies for patients and consumers.

Kansas City, known for its thriving arts scene and progressive attitudes, is another key destination for cannabis tourism. Tourists visiting Kansas City can explore the city's growing cannabis industry, including dispensaries, CBD shops, and cannabis-friendly events. Kansas City's cannabis culture is deeply intertwined with its focus on community health and wellness, making it an ideal destination for those interested in learning more about the therapeutic benefits of cannabis.

Cannabis Festivals and Events in Missouri

Missouri is home to a growing number of cannabis-themed festivals, expos, and educational events that celebrate the state's evolving cannabis market. One of the most notable events is the Missouri Medical Cannabis Conference, which brings together patients, advocates, and industry professionals to discuss the latest developments in the medical marijuana industry and explore the future of cannabis reform in Missouri.

Another popular event is the Missouri Cannabis Expo, which focuses on the potential of the cannabis industry in the state and offers a platform for business owners, entrepreneurs, and advocates to network, learn, and share insights about the growing medical cannabis market. The expo features educational panels, product showcases, and opportunities to learn about the latest innovations in cannabis technology, cultivation, and product development.

Additionally, events like the Missouri Hemp Fest have emerged, highlighting the importance of the state's hemp industry and its role in shaping the broader cannabis movement. These festivals provide a space for hemp farmers, CBD producers, and wellness advocates to connect with consumers, while also offering a range of products from hemp-derived edibles to CBD-infused topicals.

Cannabis advocacy events are also gaining traction in Missouri, with organizations like Missouri NORML hosting regular meetups and educational workshops that aim to educate the public on cannabis reform and push for the legalization of recreational cannabis. These events help build a stronger community of cannabis advocates, ensuring that the conversation around cannabis reform continues to evolve in the state.

Challenges and Opportunities in Missouri's Cannabis Market

While Missouri has made significant progress in cannabis reform with its medical marijuana program, the state still faces several challenges. One of the primary obstacles is ensuring that medical cannabis is accessible to all patients who need it, particularly those in rural areas. Missouri's medical cannabis industry is largely concentrated in major cities like St. Louis, Kansas City, and Columbia, which makes it difficult for patients in less populated areas to access dispensaries and cannabis products.

Additionally, while public support for recreational cannabis is growing, there is still resistance among some lawmakers who remain opposed to legalizing adult-use cannabis. Despite these challenges, cannabis advocates in Missouri continue to push for broader reform, and there is growing optimism that the state will eventually move toward full cannabis legalization.

Missouri's cannabis industry also presents significant opportunities for growth, particularly in areas like cannabis cultivation, dispensary operations, and product development. As the state's medical marijuana program continues to expand, there will be increasing demand for cannabis products that cater to a wide range of medical conditions. Additionally, Missouri's strong agricultural sector positions it well for hemp cultivation and CBD production, creating opportunities for farmers and entrepreneurs alike.

The Future of Cannabis in Missouri

The future of cannabis in Missouri is promising, with the state's medical marijuana program serving as a foundation for broader cannabis reform. As more Missourians experience the therapeutic benefits of medical cannabis, public support for recreational legalization is expected to grow. Advocates are hopeful that Missouri will follow the lead of other states that have successfully transitioned from medical marijuana to full adult-use legalization.

Looking ahead, Missouri has the potential to become a major player in the national cannabis industry, particularly as its medical cannabis market matures and demand for cannabis-based therapies increases. The state's growing cannabis culture, combined with its strong advocacy movement, suggests that Missouri is well on its way to becoming a leader in cannabis reform.

If Missouri ultimately legalizes recreational cannabis, the state could unlock new economic opportunities, create jobs, and provide greater access to cannabis for residents across the state. As more states across the U.S. move toward cannabis legalization, Missouri will likely face increasing pressure to join the movement and expand access to both medical and recreational cannabis.

Chapter 26: North Carolina - The Road to Cannabis Reform in the Tar Heel State

North Carolina is one of the states where cannabis reform has been slower to take root compared to others in the Southeast. While the state has made some progress in legalizing hemp and CBD products, North Carolina has yet to establish a comprehensive medical cannabis program, and recreational cannabis remains illegal. Despite these challenges, support for cannabis reform is growing among the state's residents, and advocates are pushing for changes that would allow patients greater access to medical cannabis.

North Carolina's cannabis landscape is shaped by the state's strong agricultural heritage, progressive urban centers like Charlotte, Raleigh, and Asheville, and a growing demand for natural health remedies. As more residents become aware of the therapeutic benefits of cannabis and hemp-derived products, the push for cannabis legalization is expected to gain momentum.

Hemp and CBD in North Carolina

North Carolina has been at the forefront of the hemp industry since the passage of the 2014 federal Farm Bill, which allowed for the legal cultivation of hemp for research purposes. In 2017, the state passed legislation that created a legal framework for hemp farming, making North Carolina one of the leading hemp producers in the Southeast. The state's climate and agricultural resources make it an ideal location for hemp cultivation, and North Carolina farmers have capitalized on this by growing hemp for use in CBD products and industrial applications.

The state's hemp and CBD market has grown rapidly in recent years, with CBD shops, wellness centers, and hemp farms cropping up across the state. These businesses offer a wide range of CBD-based products, including tinctures, topicals, edibles, and vape cartridges, catering to consumers seeking natural remedies for conditions like anxiety, pain, and inflammation. North Carolina's CBD market has become a thriving industry, particularly in cities like Asheville, known for its progressive and wellness-focused community.

The success of the hemp industry in North Carolina has helped normalize cannabis use, and many residents are hopeful that the state will eventually expand access to medical cannabis. Advocates continue to push for a comprehensive medical cannabis program, which they argue would provide patients with a safe and legal way to access cannabis for therapeutic purposes.

Cannabis Advocacy in North Carolina

While North Carolina's cannabis laws remain restrictive, the state is home to a growing number of cannabis advocacy groups that are working to change public opinion and push for cannabis reform. Organizations like NC NORML(National Organization for the Reform of Marijuana Laws) and the North Carolina Cannabis Patients Network have been at the forefront of efforts to educate lawmakers and the public about the benefits of medical cannabis.

Advocates in North Carolina are focused on creating a medical cannabis program that would allow patients with conditions like chronic pain, epilepsy, cancer, and PTSD to access cannabis products for relief. Many believe that the success of the state's hemp and CBD industry could pave the way for broader cannabis reform, particularly as more residents become familiar with the therapeutic benefits of cannabis.

In addition to advocating for medical cannabis, activists are also pushing for decriminalization and the eventual legalization of recreational cannabis. Although recreational legalization may be further off in North Carolina, growing public support and changing political attitudes could eventually lead to significant policy changes.

Cannabis Culture in North Carolina's Major Cities

North Carolina's cannabis culture is still in its early stages, but cities like Asheville, Charlotte, and Raleigh are leading the way in fostering a growing community of cannabis advocates, patients, and entrepreneurs. These cities are known for their progressive attitudes, focus on wellness, and support for natural health remedies, making them ideal locations for the state's emerging cannabis culture.

Asheville, nestled in the Blue Ridge Mountains, has long been known for its thriving arts scene and emphasis on holistic living. The city is home to a number of CBD shops, wellness centers, and cannabis-friendly businesses that cater to health-conscious consumers seeking natural alternatives to traditional medicine. Asheville's residents have been at the forefront of efforts to expand access to medical cannabis, and the city's cannabis culture is closely tied to its focus on community health and well-being.

Charlotte, the state's largest city, is also seeing growing support for cannabis reform. The city's residents have embraced CBD products for their therapeutic benefits, and local businesses are capitalizing on the demand for natural health remedies. Charlotte is home to a growing number of CBD retailers and wellness centers, which offer products and services designed to promote relaxation and holistic healing. As more residents become familiar with the benefits of CBD and hemp-derived products, support for cannabis reform in Charlotte is expected to increase.

In Raleigh, North Carolina's capital, cannabis culture is slowly emerging as more residents advocate for the legalization of medical cannabis. Dispensaries that sell hemp-derived products are gaining popularity in the city, and the growing number of wellness-oriented businesses reflects Raleigh's focus on promoting the health benefits of natural remedies. As the state's political center, Raleigh plays an important role in shaping cannabis policy, and local advocates are working to influence lawmakers to push for broader cannabis reform.

Cannabis Tourism in North Carolina

North Carolina's CBD market and hemp industry are attracting growing interest from tourists seeking wellness experiences and natural health remedies. Cities like Asheville and Wilmington are popular destinations for tourists looking to explore the state's scenic beauty while enjoying the benefits of CBD-based products and holistic wellness practices.

One of the most popular destinations for cannabis tourists in North Carolina is Asheville, where visitors can enjoy CBD-infused massages, hemp-friendly yoga classes, and wellness retreats that focus on promoting relaxation and healing through the use of hemp-derived products. Asheville's thriving hemp culture and its emphasis on holistic health make it an ideal destination for those interested in exploring the potential benefits of cannabis.

In addition to Asheville, cities like Wilmington and Greensboro are seeing a rise in hemp-based businesses and CBD-friendly events. Tourists visiting these cities can explore local CBD shops, hemp farms, and wellness centers, offering a unique way to experience North Carolina's evolving cannabis culture.

Cannabis Festivals and Events in North Carolina

As North Carolina's cannabis industry continues to develop, the state is seeing a growing number of hemp and CBD-themed festivals, expos, and educational events that celebrate the state's emerging cannabis market. One of the most well-known events is the Asheville Hemp Fest, which brings together hemp farmers, CBD entrepreneurs, and cannabis advocates for a weekend of music, education, and community engagement.

Another major event is the Southeast Cannabis Conference and Expo, which takes place annually in Charlotte and focuses on the future of the hemp and cannabis industries in North Carolina and the broader Southeast. The conference features educational panels, product displays, and networking opportunities for industry professionals, patients, and advocates interested in the latest trends and developments in the cannabis market.

In addition to these larger events, North Carolina is home to a growing number of CBD-friendly pop-up markets, wellness retreats, and educational workshops that promote the health benefits of hemp and cannabis. These events provide consumers with an opportunity to learn more about the therapeutic uses of cannabis and connect with others in the community.

Challenges and Opportunities in North Carolina's Cannabis Market

While North Carolina's cannabis market is still in its early stages, the state faces several challenges, particularly in terms of regulatory barriers and limited access to cannabis products. The lack of a comprehensive medical cannabis program prevents many patients from accessing cannabis for therapeutic use, and the state's conservative political climate has made it difficult to pass cannabis reform legislation.

However, North Carolina's hemp industry and CBD market offer significant opportunities for growth, particularly in areas like hemp cultivation, product development, and wellness tourism. As demand for hemp-derived products continues to grow, North Carolina's agricultural sector is well-positioned to become a leader in the national hemp industry.

The Future of Cannabis in North Carolina

The future of cannabis in North Carolina will depend on continued advocacy efforts and changes in public opinion. As more North Carolinians become aware of the therapeutic benefits of cannabis, there is hope that the state will eventually adopt a medical cannabis program that allows patients to access cannabis for a broader range of conditions.

The state's growing hemp industry and CBD market will continue to play an important role in shaping the future of cannabis in North Carolina. With its strong agricultural base and commitment to natural health remedies, North Carolina has the potential to become a key player in the national hemp and CBD markets.

If North Carolina eventually legalizes medical or recreational cannabis, the state could unlock new economic opportunities, create jobs, and provide greater access to cannabis for residents across the state. As more states across the U.S. move toward legalization, North Carolina will likely face increasing pressure to join the movement and expand access to cannabis for both medical and recreational use.

Chapter 27: Wisconsin - A Conservative State with Growing Support for Medical Cannabis

Wisconsin, historically known for its conservative stance on cannabis, is seeing growing public support for the legalization of medical marijuana. While recreational cannabis remains illegal and the state's laws regarding marijuana possession and use are among the strictest in the nation, there is increasing pressure from residents and advocates to establish a medical cannabis program. Neighboring states like Illinois and Michigan have fully embraced cannabis reform, leaving Wisconsin one of the few holdouts in the region.

In recent years, there has been a growing movement in Wisconsin advocating for medical cannabis legalization, as more residents recognize the therapeutic benefits of cannabis for conditions like chronic pain, anxiety, PTSD, and cancer. As public opinion shifts, cities like Madison, Milwaukee, and Green Bay are becoming hubs for cannabis advocacy, with residents pushing for broader access to medical marijuana.

Cannabis Advocacy in Wisconsin

The fight for medical cannabis reform in Wisconsin has been led by a coalition of patients, advocacy groups, and healthcare professionals who argue that patients with debilitating conditions should have access to medical marijuana. Organizations like Wisconsin NORML (National Organization for the Reform of Marijuana Laws) and the Wisconsin Cannabis Association have been instrumental in educating the public and lobbying lawmakers to pass legislation that would establish a comprehensive medical marijuana program in the state.

Despite these efforts, Wisconsin lawmakers have been slow to embrace cannabis reform. Several attempts to pass medical cannabis legislation have stalled in the state legislature, with opposition from conservative politicians who remain skeptical about the benefits of cannabis. However, advocates are hopeful that as more states move toward cannabis legalization, Wisconsin will eventually follow suit.

Polling data suggests that a majority of Wisconsin residents support the legalization of medical marijuana, and there is growing frustration among patients and advocates over the state's slow progress. Many residents have expressed concerns about having to travel to neighboring states like Illinois or Michigan to access medical cannabis products, highlighting the need for reform in Wisconsin.

The CBD and Hemp Market in Wisconsin

While marijuana remains illegal in Wisconsin, the state has embraced the production of hemp and CBD products following the passage of the 2018 Farm Bill, which legalized the cultivation of industrial hemp. Wisconsin has a long agricultural history, and the state's farmers have capitalized on the growing demand for hemp-derived products by cultivating hemp for CBD extraction and other uses.

The success of the CBD market in Wisconsin has helped normalize cannabis use for many residents, even as the state maintains its restrictive stance on marijuana. CBD products, including tinctures, edibles, topicals, and vape products, are widely available across Wisconsin and have become popular among consumers seeking natural remedies for conditions like chronic pain, anxiety, and sleep disorders.

In cities like Madison and Milwaukee, the CBD industry is thriving, with CBD shops, wellness centers, and hemp farms offering a wide range of products that cater to consumers interested in natural health remedies. The success of the CBD industry in Wisconsin has paved the way for broader conversations about the therapeutic benefits of cannabis, and many advocates see CBD legalization as a stepping stone toward medical cannabis reform.

Cannabis Culture in Wisconsin's Major Cities

Wisconsin's cannabis culture is emerging in cities like Madison, Milwaukee, and Green Bay, where residents are increasingly advocating for cannabis reform and embracing CBD products as a natural alternative to traditional medicine. These cities are home to thriving CBD markets, with CBD retailers, hemp farms, and wellness businesses contributing to the state's evolving cannabis landscape.

Madison, the state capital and home to the University of Wisconsin-Madison, has become a hub for cannabis advocacy and entrepreneurship. The city's progressive attitudes and focus on health and wellness have made it a focal point for Wisconsin's CBD industry, with numerous CBD retailers offering a wide range of products designed to promote relaxation and pain relief. Madison's residents are at the forefront of efforts to push for medical cannabis legalization, and the city's cannabis culture is closely tied to its emphasis on natural health remedies.

Milwaukee, Wisconsin's largest city, is also seeing growing support for cannabis reform. The city's CBD shops and wellness centers have become popular destinations for residents seeking relief from a variety of health conditions, and Milwaukee's community-driven approach to health and wellness has helped foster a supportive environment for cannabis reform.

Green Bay, known for its sports culture and outdoor lifestyle, is another key player in Wisconsin's cannabis movement. The city's residents are increasingly turning to CBD products as a natural alternative to pharmaceuticals, and Green Bay's cannabis culture is closely aligned with its focus on health, fitness, and community well-being.

Cannabis Tourism in Wisconsin

While recreational cannabis is illegal in Wisconsin, the state's CBD market and hemp industry are attracting visitors interested in wellness tourism and natural health remedies. Cities like Madison and Milwaukee offer tourists access to a growing number of CBD shops, hemp farms, and wellness centers, providing a unique way for visitors to experience Wisconsin's emerging cannabis culture.

Madison is a popular destination for tourists seeking CBD-friendly experiences, with many local businesses offering CBD-infused products, CBD massages, and hemp-based skincare products. Visitors to Madison can enjoy the city's vibrant culture while exploring its cannabis culture, which is centered around the therapeutic benefits of hemp-derived products.

In addition to its urban attractions, Wisconsin is home to a growing hemp farming industry, which offers potential opportunities for hemp farm tours and educational experiences that teach visitors about the cultivation and processing of hemp for CBD extraction and other industrial applications.

Cannabis Festivals and Events in Wisconsin

Wisconsin is seeing a rise in hemp and CBD-themed festivals, expos, and educational events that celebrate the state's evolving cannabis market. One of the most notable events is the Wisconsin Hemp Expo, which brings together farmers, entrepreneurs, and advocates to discuss the latest developments in the hemp and CBD industries.

Another popular event is the Midwest Cannabis Business Conference, which focuses on the potential of cannabis in the Midwest region, including Wisconsin. The conference features educational panels, product showcases, and networking opportunities for those involved in the hemp and CBD markets.

Challenges and Opportunities in Wisconsin's Cannabis Market

Wisconsin's cannabis market faces several challenges, particularly in terms of regulatory barriers and the lack of a medical cannabis program. While the state's CBD industry has flourished, the absence of a comprehensive medical marijuana program has left many patients without access to cannabis products that could improve their quality of life. Additionally, Wisconsin's conservative political climate presents obstacles to broader cannabis reform.

Despite these challenges, Wisconsin's hemp industry offers significant opportunities for growth, particularly in areas like hemp cultivation, CBD product development, and wellness tourism. As demand for CBD products continues to grow, Wisconsin is well-positioned to become a leader in the national hemp market, creating opportunities for farmers, entrepreneurs, and retailers.

The Future of Cannabis in Wisconsin

The future of cannabis in Wisconsin will depend largely on continued advocacy efforts and changes in public opinion. As more Wisconsinites become aware of the therapeutic benefits of cannabis, there is growing support for the establishment of a comprehensive medical cannabis program. Advocates are hopeful that state lawmakers will recognize the need for cannabis reform and pass legislation that allows patients to access medical cannabis for a broader range of conditions.

The state's growing hemp industry and CBD market will continue to play an important role in shaping the future of cannabis in Wisconsin. With its strong agricultural base and favorable conditions for hemp farming, Wisconsin is well-positioned to capitalize on the booming hemp market, offering opportunities for local businesses and farmers to thrive.

Looking ahead, Wisconsin may eventually consider the legalization of recreational cannabis, particularly as neighboring states move toward cannabis reform. If Wisconsin fully embraces cannabis legalization, the state could unlock new economic opportunities, create jobs, and provide greater access to cannabis for residents across the state.

Chapter 28: Ohio - Medical Marijuana and the Journey Toward Full Legalization

Ohio has taken significant steps in cannabis reform, particularly with the establishment of a comprehensive medical marijuana program. While the state has yet to legalize recreational cannabis, Ohio's medical marijuana market has grown rapidly since its launch, offering patients access to a wide range of cannabis products. As more Ohioans recognize the therapeutic benefits of cannabis, the push for broader cannabis reform, including recreational legalization, continues to gain momentum.

Ohio's medical marijuana program, established in 2016 with the passage of House Bill 523, allows patients with qualifying conditions to purchase cannabis from state-licensed dispensaries. Cities like Columbus, Cleveland, and Cincinnati have become key locations for Ohio's growing cannabis culture, with dispensaries and cannabis-friendly events contributing to the state's evolving market. As the state's medical cannabis industry expands, many advocates believe that Ohio is on the path toward full adult-use legalization.

The Establishment of Medical Marijuana in Ohio

In 2016, Ohio became the 25th state to legalize medical marijuana with the passage of House Bill 523, which created a legal framework for the cultivation, production, and sale of medical cannabis. The bill allows patients with qualifying conditions, such as chronic pain, PTSD, epilepsy, and multiple sclerosis, to purchase cannabis from licensed dispensaries. Patients must obtain a recommendation from a certified physician and register with the state to obtain a medical marijuana card.

The state's medical marijuana program has grown rapidly since its launch, with thousands of patients enrolling each year and dozens of dispensaries opening across Ohio. The program is considered one of the most successful in the Midwest, providing patients with access to high-quality cannabis products that help manage a wide range of medical conditions.

The Dispensary Scene in Ohio

Ohio's dispensary scene is flourishing, with licensed medical marijuana dispensaries operating in cities across the state. Columbus, Cleveland, and Cincinnati have become major hubs for Ohio's medical cannabis industry, offering patients access to a variety of cannabis products that cater to their specific medical needs.

Columbus, the state capital and largest city, has emerged as a key player in Ohio's cannabis market. The city is home to numerous medical marijuana dispensaries, where patients can purchase cannabis-based therapies for conditions like chronic pain, anxiety, and epilepsy. Columbus' growing cannabis culture is tied to its focus on health and wellness, with local businesses providing educational resources on the therapeutic benefits of cannabis.

Cleveland, located along Lake Erie, has also embraced Ohio's medical marijuana program, with dispensaries providing patients with access to a wide range of cannabis products. Cleveland's residents are increasingly turning to medical cannabis for relief from chronic conditions, and the city's cannabis culture is becoming a focal point for efforts to expand access to both medical and recreational cannabis.

In Cincinnati, a city known for its rich cultural history and vibrant arts scene, medical marijuana dispensaries have become popular destinations for residents seeking natural health remedies. Cincinnati's cannabis community is active and engaged, with local advocates pushing for further reforms that would allow for the legalization of recreational cannabis.

Cannabis Advocacy in Ohio

Ohio's cannabis reform movement has been driven by a coalition of patients, advocates, and organizations dedicated to expanding access to medical cannabis and pushing for the legalization of recreational cannabis. Groups like Ohio NORML (National Organization for the Reform of Marijuana Laws) and Ohio Patients Network have played a key role in educating the public about the therapeutic benefits of cannabis and advocating for broader cannabis reform in the state.

Advocates argue that the success of Ohio's medical marijuana program is evidence that the state is ready for adult-use legalization. Polling data suggests that a majority of Ohio residents support the legalization of recreational cannabis, and there is growing pressure on state lawmakers to pass legislation that would allow adults over the age of 21 to purchase and use cannabis for recreational purposes.

In addition to advocating for recreational cannabis legalization, advocates are working to improve Ohio's medical marijuana program, particularly in the areas of patient access and affordability. While the program is considered successful, there are concerns about the cost of medical cannabis products and the availability of dispensaries in rural areas. Advocates are calling for reforms that would make medical cannabis more accessible to patients across the state.

Cannabis Culture in Ohio's Major Cities

Ohio's cannabis culture is rapidly evolving, particularly in cities like Columbus, Cleveland, and Cincinnati, where medical marijuana dispensaries and cannabis-friendly events are becoming more common. These cities are home to thriving cannabis communities, with local businesses, advocates, and patients working together to promote the therapeutic benefits of cannabis and push for broader cannabis reform.

Columbus, with its growing population and vibrant arts scene, has embraced the medical cannabis industry, with numerous dispensaries and wellness centers offering products designed to improve health and well-being. The city's cannabis culture is closely tied to its focus on community health, with many local businesses offering educational resources on the use of medical cannabis for conditions like chronic pain, anxiety, and PTSD.

Cleveland, known for its diverse culture and progressive values, has become a key player in Ohio's cannabis reform movement. The city's medical cannabis dispensaries provide patients with access to a wide range of cannabis-based therapies, and Cleveland's residents are increasingly advocating for the legalization of recreational cannabis. The city's cannabis culture is deeply rooted in its focus on wellness and community engagement.

In Cincinnati, with its emphasis on arts and culture, the cannabis community is growing as more residents turn to medical marijuana for relief from a variety of conditions. The city's dispensaries provide patients with access to high-quality cannabis products, and local advocacy groups are working to expand access to both medical and recreational cannabis.

Cannabis Tourism in Ohio

While recreational cannabis is not yet legal in Ohio, the state's medical marijuana program and CBD market are attracting visitors interested in wellness tourism and natural health remedies. Cities like Columbus, Cleveland, and Cincinnati offer tourists access to medical cannabis dispensaries, CBD shops, and cannabis-friendly wellness centers, providing a unique way for visitors to experience Ohio's emerging cannabis culture.

Columbus, with its vibrant cultural scene and progressive attitudes, is a popular destination for cannabis tourists seeking medical cannabis or CBD-infused products. Visitors to Columbus can explore the city's numerous dispensaries and wellness centers, which offer a variety of cannabis-based therapies for patients and consumers.

Cleveland, with its reputation as a cultural hub and medical center, is also attracting cannabis tourists who are interested in learning more about the state's medical marijuana program. Visitors to Cleveland can tour the city's medical cannabis dispensaries and explore its cannabis-friendly events, gaining insight into the therapeutic benefits of cannabis for conditions like chronic pain and anxiety.

Cannabis Festivals and Events in Ohio

Ohio is home to a growing number of cannabis-themed festivals, expos, and educational events that celebrate the state's evolving cannabis market. One of the most notable events is the Ohio Cannabis Health Summit, which brings together patients.

Chapter 29: Iowa - A Conservative State's Push Toward Cannabis Reform

Iowa, a deeply conservative state in the Midwest, has been slower than many other states in adopting cannabis reform. However, despite its traditionally conservative stance, there is growing momentum for change as more residents recognize the potential benefits of medical cannabis and hemp-derived products. Iowa currently has a limited medical cannabidiol (CBD) program, which allows for the use of CBD products containing up to 3% THC for patients with qualifying conditions. The state also has a burgeoning hemp industry, which is contributing to a shift in public perception around cannabis use.

While Iowa's cannabis laws remain restrictive, the conversation around cannabis reform is evolving. Advocates are working to expand the state's medical cannabis program and push for recreational cannabis legalization, as more Iowans call for greater access to cannabis products for both medical and adult use. Cities like Des Moines, Cedar Rapids, and Iowa City are leading the charge, with CBD shops, hemp farms, and wellness centers contributing to the state's growing interest in cannabis.

Iowa's Medical Cannabidiol Program

Iowa's current medical cannabidiol (CBD) program is limited in scope but represents a significant step toward broader cannabis reform. The program, established in 2014 and expanded in subsequent years, allows patients with qualifying conditions, such as chronic pain, epilepsy, Parkinson's disease, and multiple sclerosis, to access CBD products with up to 3% THC content. Patients must receive a recommendation from a licensed physician and apply for a medical cannabidiol card through the Iowa Department of Public Health.

Despite the progress made with Iowa's CBD program, many patients and advocates argue that the state's restrictions on THC content limit the effectiveness of cannabis for treating severe conditions. The 3% THC cap, in particular, has been a point of contention, as it prevents patients from accessing full-strength cannabis products that may provide more substantial relief. Advocates continue to push for reforms that would expand access to medical cannabis and allow for higher THC concentrations.

Additionally, Iowa's CBD program faces challenges related to accessibility and availability. Currently, there are only a few licensed dispensaries across the state, making it difficult for patients in rural areas to access cannabidiol products. Advocates are calling for the expansion of the medical cannabis program to ensure that patients in all parts of Iowa have access to cannabis-based therapies.

The Role of Hemp and CBD in Iowa's Cannabis Market

The 2018 Farm Bill paved the way for hemp cultivation in Iowa, and the state has embraced the opportunity to develop a thriving hemp industry. Iowa's farmers are increasingly turning to hemp production as a way to diversify their crops and meet the growing demand for CBD products and hemp-derived materials. The state's agricultural heritage and fertile soil make it an ideal location for hemp farming, and Iowa is quickly becoming a leader in the Midwest hemp market.

As more Iowans turn to CBD products for their therapeutic benefits, public support for broader cannabis reform is growing. The success of the state's hemp market has also created new economic opportunities for farmers and entrepreneurs, positioning Iowa as a key player in the national hemp and CBD industries.

Cannabis Advocacy in Iowa

Advocacy for cannabis reform in Iowa has gained momentum in recent years, with organizations like Iowa NORML and Iowa Cannabis Coalition leading the charge. These groups are working to expand Iowa's medical CBD program and push for recreational cannabis legalization, arguing that patients and consumers deserve greater access to cannabis-based therapies.

Advocates have been particularly vocal about the need to raise the THC cap in Iowa's medical cannabidiol program. Many patients with chronic or debilitating conditions have expressed frustration with the state's current restrictions, which they argue prevent them from accessing the full benefits of medical cannabis. Advocates are calling for legislation that would allow for higher THC concentrations in medical cannabis products, bringing Iowa in line with other states that have more comprehensive medical marijuana programs.

In addition to advocating for medical cannabis reform, activists are also pushing for the decriminalization of cannabis possession. Under current Iowa law, possession of even small amounts of cannabis is a criminal offense that can result in severe penalties, including fines and jail time. Advocacy groups are working to reduce the penalties for cannabis possession, particularly for nonviolent offenses, and are calling for decriminalization measures that would make it easier for individuals to avoid criminal charges for minor offenses.

Cannabis Culture in Iowa's Major Cities

While Iowa's cannabis laws remain restrictive, the state's cannabis culture is slowly emerging, particularly in cities like Des Moines, Cedar Rapids, and Iowa City, where CBD products are widely available and residents are increasingly advocating for cannabis reform. These cities are home to thriving CBD markets, with CBD shops, hemp farms, and wellness centers contributing to the state's evolving cannabis scene.

Des Moines, the capital and largest city in Iowa, has become a hub for cannabis advocates and entrepreneurs. The city's CBD shops and wellness centers offer a wide range of hemp-derived products, catering to residents seeking natural remedies for pain relief, anxiety, and sleep disorders. Des Moines' residents are also at the forefront of efforts to push for medical cannabis reform, and the city's CBD culture is closely tied to its focus on health and wellness.

Cedar Rapids, the second-largest city in Iowa, has also embraced the potential of CBD products. The city's CBD shops and hemp farms have become popular destinations for residents seeking natural health remedies, and Cedar Rapids' community-driven approach to wellness has helped foster a supportive environment for cannabis reform.

In Iowa City, home to the University of Iowa, cannabis culture is thriving as more residents turn to CBD products for relief from a variety of conditions. The city's progressive attitudes and emphasis on wellness have made it a focal point for efforts to expand access to medical cannabis and push for recreational legalization.

Cannabis Tourism in Iowa

Although recreational cannabis is not yet legal in Iowa, the state's CBD market and hemp industry are attracting visitors interested in wellness tourism and natural health remedies. Cities like Des Moines and Iowa City offer tourists access to a growing number of CBD shops, wellness centers, and hemp farms, providing a unique way for visitors to experience Iowa's emerging cannabis culture.

Des Moines is a popular destination for tourists seeking CBD-friendly experiences, with many local businesses offering CBD-infused products, CBD massages, and hemp-based skincare products. Visitors to Des Moines can explore the city's wellness culture while learning about the therapeutic benefits of hemp-derived products.

Iowa City, with its vibrant college atmosphere and progressive values, also offers tourists a chance to explore Iowa's emerging CBD market. Visitors can enjoy the city's CBD shops and hemp-friendly events, which highlight the growing demand for hemp-derived products in Iowa.

Cannabis Festivals and Events in Iowa

Iowa is home to a growing number of hemp and CBD-themed festivals, expos, and educational events that celebrate the state's evolving cannabis market. One of the most notable events is the Iowa Hemp Expo, which brings together farmers, entrepreneurs, and advocates to discuss the latest developments in the hemp and CBD industries.

The Iowa Hemp Expo features educational panels, product showcases, and networking opportunities for those involved in the hemp and CBD markets. It is an important event for those looking to gain insights into Iowa's growing hemp industry and explore the potential for future cannabis reform.

In addition to these larger events, Iowa hosts a variety of CBD-friendly pop-up markets, wellness retreats, and educational workshops that promote the health benefits of hemp-derived products. These events provide residents and visitors with the opportunity to learn more about the therapeutic uses of cannabis and connect with local CBD businesses.

Challenges and Opportunities in Iowa's Cannabis Market

Iowa's cannabis market faces several challenges, particularly in terms of accessibility and the limited scope of the state's medical cannabidiol (CBD) program. The state's strict THC cap on medical cannabis products and the limited number of licensed dispensaries make it difficult for many patients to access the full benefits of cannabis-based therapies. Additionally, the conservative political climate in Iowa presents obstacles to broader cannabis reform, as many lawmakers remain opposed to recreational legalization and the expansion of medical cannabis access.

Despite these challenges, Iowa's hemp industry and CBD market offer significant opportunities for growth. The state's agricultural heritage and favorable climate for hemp farming make Iowa an ideal location for the expansion of the hemp market, which could provide new economic opportunities for farmers, entrepreneurs, and local businesses. As demand for CBD products continues to grow, Iowa is well-positioned to become a leader in the Midwestern hemp market, helping to shape the future of cannabis reform in the state.

The Future of Cannabis in Iowa

The future of cannabis reform in Iowa depends on continued advocacy efforts and changes in public opinion. As more Iowans become aware of the therapeutic benefits of cannabis, there is growing support for the expansion of the state's medical cannabis program and the legalization of recreational cannabis. Advocates are hopeful that state lawmakers will recognize the need for cannabis reform and pass legislation that allows patients and consumers to access a broader range of cannabis products.

Iowa's growing hemp industry and CBD market will continue to play an important role in shaping the future of cannabis reform in the state. With its strong agricultural base and increasing demand for hemp-derived products, Iowa is well-positioned to capitalize on the booming hemp market, offering opportunities for local businesses, farmers, and entrepreneurs to thrive.

Looking ahead, Iowa may eventually consider the legalization of recreational cannabis, particularly as neighboring states move toward cannabis reform. If Iowa fully embraces cannabis legalization, the state could unlock new economic opportunities, create jobs, and provide greater access to cannabis for residents across the state.

Chapter 30: Arkansas - Medical Marijuana and the Challenges of Southern Cannabis Reform

Arkansas, a conservative Southern state, made a significant leap toward cannabis reform with the legalization of medical marijuana through Amendment 98, also known as the Arkansas Medical Marijuana Amendment, in 2016. Despite its conservative political landscape, the state has embraced medical cannabis, providing patients with access to a wide range of cannabis-based therapies. However, Arkansas faces significant challenges in terms of the slow rollout of dispensaries, high taxes, and strict regulatory oversight.

While recreational cannabis remains illegal, Arkansas' growing medical marijuana industry has opened the door for future discussions about broader cannabis reform. Cities like Little Rock, Fayetteville, and Fort Smith are becoming centers of Arkansas' medical marijuana market, with dispensaries providing access to cannabis products and a growing community of cannabis advocates pushing for further legalization.

The Passage of Medical Marijuana in Arkansas

In 2016, Arkansas voters passed Amendment 98, which legalized medical cannabis for patients with qualifying conditions such as chronic pain, PTSD, epilepsy, and cancer. The amendment established a legal framework for the cultivation, production, and distribution of medical cannabis in the state. Under the law, patients can purchase medical cannabis products from state-licensed dispensaries after obtaining a medical marijuana card from a certified physician.

The Dispensary Scene in Arkansas

Arkansas' medical marijuana dispensary scene is slowly growing, with licensed dispensaries opening across the state in cities like Little Rock, Fayetteville, and Fort Smith. These dispensaries provide patients with access to a variety of cannabis products for treating their medical conditions.

Little Rock, the capital of Arkansas, has become a focal point for the state's medical marijuana industry, with several dispensaries offering patients a range of cannabis-based therapies. The city's cannabis culture is still developing, but medical cannabis has become a popular alternative for patients seeking natural remedies for chronic conditions. Fayetteville, home to the University of Arkansas, is another important location for Arkansas' cannabis industry, with dispensaries catering to the needs of patients in the region. Fort Smith has also seen the growth of dispensaries, helping to expand access to medical cannabis in western Arkansas.

Cannabis Advocacy in Arkansas

Cannabis advocacy in Arkansas has been led by groups like Arkansas NORML and Arkansans for Compassionate Care, which played key roles in the passage of Amendment 98 and continue to push for the expansion of the state's medical marijuana program. Advocates are working to reduce the costs associated with medical cannabis and to ensure that dispensaries are more accessible to patients in rural areas of the state.

While recreational cannabis remains a distant goal for many advocates, there is growing support among Arkansas residents for the legalization of adult-use cannabis. Advocates argue that the success of the state's medical marijuana program is evidence that Arkansas is ready for broader cannabis reform. Recent polls suggest that a significant portion of Arkansas residents support recreational legalization, although the state's conservative political climate remains a challenge.

Cannabis Culture in Arkansas' Major Cities

Although Arkansas' cannabis culture is still in its early stages, cities like Little Rock, Fayetteville, and Fort Smith are seeing growing interest in medical cannabis as a treatment option for a variety of conditions. Dispensaries in these cities offer patients access to high-quality cannabis products, and local cannabis advocates continue to push for broader access and reform.

Little Rock, the state's largest city, has become a hub for medical cannabis patients and advocates. Dispensaries in the city offer a range of products to help patients manage conditions like chronic pain, PTSD, and anxiety. Little Rock's cannabis culture is beginning to take shape, with growing support for cannabis reform and an increasing number of residents turning to medical marijuana as an alternative to prescription medications.

Fayetteville, with its youthful and progressive population, is also seeing the growth of a cannabis culture centered around medical marijuana. The city's dispensaries provide patients with access to a variety of cannabis-based therapies, and cannabis-friendly businesses are starting to emerge in the area. As the medical cannabis industry continues to grow, Fayetteville is expected to play an important role in shaping the future of cannabis reform in Arkansas.

Cannabis Tourism in Arkansas

Although recreational cannabis remains illegal in Arkansas, the state's medical marijuana program and CBD industry are starting to attract visitors interested in wellness tourism and natural health remedies. Visitors to cities like Little Rock and Fayetteville can explore the state's growing medical cannabis market, visiting dispensaries and wellness centers that offer a variety of cannabis-based therapies.

Little Rock is emerging as a destination for cannabis tourism, with local dispensaries and CBD shops providing access to a wide range of cannabis products. Tourists visiting Little Rock can learn more about medical cannabis and its therapeutic benefits while enjoying the city's cultural and historical attractions. Fayetteville also offers tourists the chance to explore Arkansas' medical cannabis industry, with dispensaries providing patients and visitors access to natural health remedies.

Cannabis Festivals and Events in Arkansas

Arkansas is home to a growing number of cannabis-themed festivals, expos, and educational events that celebrate the state's evolving medical cannabis market. One of the most notable events is the Arkansas Cannabis Industry Association Conference, which brings together patients,advocates, and industry professionals to discuss the latest developments in the medical cannabis industry and explore the future of cannabis reform in Arkansas.

Another popular event is the Arkansas Hemp Festival, which focuses on the state's hemp and CBD industries and offers educational resources for residents interested in learning more about the therapeutic uses of hemp. The festival features product displays, educational panels, and networking opportunities for those involved in the cannabis industry.

Challenges and Opportunities in Arkansas' Cannabis Market

Arkansas' cannabis market faces several challenges, particularly in terms of regulatory hurdles and the limited number of dispensaries. While the state's medical marijuana program has expanded access to cannabis-based therapies, the slow rollout of dispensaries and high taxes on cannabis products have made it difficult for some patients to obtain the care they need.

Despite these challenges, Arkansas' medical cannabis industry offers significant opportunities for growth, particularly as demand for cannabis products continues to rise. As more patients enroll in the state's medical marijuana program, there are opportunities for dispensaries, cultivators, and processors to thrive in Arkansas' cannabis market.

The Future of Cannabis in Arkansas

The future of cannabis in Arkansas is full of potential, particularly as the state's medical marijuana program continues to grow. Advocates are hopeful that Arkansas will eventually embrace recreational cannabis legalization, which would open up new economic opportunities, create jobs, and provide greater access to cannabis products for residents across the state.

Looking ahead, Arkansas' hemp industry and CBD market will also play an important role in shaping the future of cannabis reform in the state. With its agricultural base and growing demand for hemp-derived products, Arkansas is well-positioned to capitalize on the national hemp market, offering opportunities for local businesses and farmers.

Chapter 31: Oklahoma - The Medical Marijuana Frontier

Oklahoma is one of the most surprising success stories in the U.S. cannabis reform movement. Despite its conservative reputation, Oklahoma's voters passed State Question 788 in 2018, legalizing medical marijuana with one of the most progressive and accessible programs in the country. Since then, Oklahoma has become home to a booming medical cannabis industry, with more than 10% of the state's population registered as medical marijuana patients.

The state's medical marijuana program has grown rapidly, with thousands of licensed dispensaries, cultivators, and processors operating across Oklahoma. Oklahoma City, Tulsa, and Norman are at the center of the state's thriving cannabis market, offering patients access to a wide variety of cannabis products. While recreational cannabis remains illegal, Oklahoma's success with medical marijuana has prompted discussions about broader cannabis reform.

Oklahoma's Medical Marijuana Program

Oklahoma's medical marijuana program is one of the most patient-friendly in the nation. Unlike many other states, Oklahoma does not have a set list of qualifying conditions for medical marijuana. Instead, patients can obtain a medical marijuana recommendation from a licensed physician for any condition that they and their doctor agree would benefit from cannabis treatment. This flexibility has made Oklahoma's program one of the most accessible in the U.S., leading to a significant increase in patient registrations.

Since the passage of State Question 788, Oklahoma's medical marijuana program has grown rapidly. The Oklahoma Medical Marijuana Authority (OMMA) oversees the program, issuing licenses to dispensaries, cultivators, and processors. With more than 2,000 licensed dispensaries and thousands of licensed growers, Oklahoma has one of the most robust cannabis markets in the country.

Cannabis Culture in Oklahoma's Major Cities

Oklahoma's cannabis culture is flourishing, particularly in cities like Oklahoma City, Tulsa, and Norman, where medical marijuana dispensaries are widely available and cannabis use is becoming increasingly normalized.

Tulsa, the second-largest city in Oklahoma, is another key location for the state's cannabis industry. Dispensaries in Tulsa provide patients with access to high-quality cannabis products, and the city's growing cannabis community is working to expand access to cannabis for both medical and recreational use. Tulsa's progressive attitudes and strong sense of community make it an ideal location for the state's cannabis reform movement.

In Norman, home to the University of Oklahoma, cannabis culture is steadily growing as more residents and students advocate for broader cannabis reform. Dispensaries in Norman offer patients access to cannabis-based therapies, and the city's progressive values have made it a focal point for efforts to expand access to both medical and recreational cannabis.

Chapter 32: South Carolina - A Slow Path to Cannabis Reform

South Carolina, a state with deep conservative roots, has been slow to embrace cannabis reform. While neighboring states have made significant strides in legalizing medical marijuana and even recreational cannabis, South Carolina continues to maintain some of the most restrictive cannabis laws in the country. Both medical and recreational cannabis remain illegal, and penalties for cannabis possession can be severe. However, there are signs that public opinion is slowly shifting, and advocates are pushing for broader cannabis reform in the state.

Although South Carolina has yet to legalize medical marijuana, the state has allowed the sale of CBD products and hemp-derived products under the 2014 Farm Bill, which has helped to normalize cannabis in some parts of the state. Cities like Charleston, Columbia, and Greenville are becoming hubs for CBD culture and hemp-based welness, with local businesses contributing to the evolving conversation around cannabis reform.

Hemp and CBD in South Carolina

Cities like Charleston, Columbia, and Greenville have become focal points for South Carolina's emerging CBD culture, with local businesses offering a range of hemp-based products to residents and tourists alike. South Carolina's hemp industry has helped to normalize the use of cannabis-derived products, and many advocates believe that the success of the CBD market could serve as a stepping stone toward broader cannabis reform in the state.

Cannabis Advocacy in South Carolina

Advocates argue that patients with debilitating conditions, such as chronic pain, PTSD, epilepsy, and cancer, deserve access to medical cannabis as a safe and effective treatment option. While South Carolina allows limited access to CBD oil for patients with intractable epilepsy, the state does not yet have a full medical marijuana program. Activists continue to push for legislation that would allow more patients to access medical cannabis for a wider range of conditions.

One of the key pieces of legislation being advocated for is the Compassionate Care Act, which would create a legal framework for the use of medical cannabis in South Carolina. The bill has gained support in recent years, but it has yet to pass in the state legislature. Advocates remain hopeful that with continued public pressure and education, South Carolina will eventually join the growing number of states that have embraced medical cannabis.

Cannabis Culture in South Carolina's Major Cities

Charleston, known for its historic charm and vibrant cultural scene, has become a hub for CBD culture in South Carolina. The city is home to numerous CBD shops and hemp-friendly businesses that cater to both residents and tourists seeking natural health remedies. As more Charlestonians turn to CBD products for relief from conditions like anxiety and chronic pain, the city is expected to play a key role in pushing for broader cannabis reform in the state.

Columbia, the state capital, is another key player in South Carolina's evolving cannabis landscape. The city's CBD retailers and wellness centers have become popular destinations for residents seeking natural remedies, and Columbia's residents are at the forefront of efforts to push for medical cannabis legalization. As the state's cannabis culture evolves, Columbia is expected to play an important role in shaping the future of cannabis policy in South Carolina.

Greenville, located in the foothills of the Blue Ridge Mountains, has also seen growing support for cannabis reform. The city's CBD shops and wellness businesses offer a wide range of hemp-derived products, and residents are increasingly advocating for access to medical cannabis. Greenville's focus on health and wellness makes it a natural fit for the state's emerging cannabis culture, and the city is likely to play an important role in the push for broader cannabis legalization in South Carolina.

Cannabis Tourism in South Carolina

Although recreational cannabis is not yet legal in South Carolina, the state's CBD industry and hemp farms are beginning to attract visitors interested in wellness tourism and natural health remedies. Charleston and Myrtle Beach are two popular destinations for tourists seeking to explore South Carolina's scenic beauty while enjoying the benefits of hemp-derived products.

In Charleston, visitors can participate in CBD-infused spa treatments, wellness retreats, and hemp-friendly yoga classes, while also exploring the city's rich history and vibrant culinary scene.

Chapter 33 Kansas The Fight for Cannabis Legalization in the Heartland

Kansas has long been known for its conservative values and its resistance to cannabis reform In a state where even medical marijuana remains illegal the fight for cannabis legalization has been an uphill battle for advocates. Despite these challenges there is growing support for cannabis reform particularly among younger generations and progressive communities in cities like Wichita Lawrence and Kansas City.

The road to legalization in Kansas has been met with significant opposition from lawmakers and law enforcement agencies. However advocates have been persistent in their efforts to educate the public and push for change Kansas is one of the few remaining states where cannabis is completely prohibited making it a focal point for national cannabis advocacy organizations that are working to bring reform to every state in the country.

In recent years Kansas has seen a rise in support for medical marijuana with residents calling for access to cannabis for patients suffering from debilitating conditions such as chronic pain epilepsy and cancer. Advocates argue that medical marijuana could provide a safe and effective alternative to prescription medications particularly opioids which have contributed to the state's ongoing opioid crisis.

Despite public support for medical marijuana reform efforts in the Kansas legislature have stalled Lawmakers have introduced several bills aimed at legalizing medical marijuana but these efforts have been blocked by conservative legislators who argue that cannabis poses a risk to public health and safety As a result Kansas remains one of the last states without a medical marijuana program.

However there is hope for the future of cannabis in Kansas With neighboring states like Missouri and Colorado embracing cannabis reform Kansas residents are increasingly supportive of legalization. As more states move toward legalizing both medical and recreational cannabis there is growing pressure on Kansas lawmakers to follow suit. Advocates are hopeful that Kansas will eventually join the movement and expand access to cannabis for both medical and recreational use.

Chapter 34 Nebraska A Conservative States Resistance to Cannabis Reform

Nebraska like its neighbor Kansas is one of the few remaining states where cannabis is fully prohibited Despite growing support for cannabis reform in the state Nebraska's conservative political landscape has made it difficult for advocates to push for meaningful change. Both medical and recreational cannabis remain illegal and possession of even small amounts of cannabis is punishable by fines or jail time.

In recent years Nebraska has seen several efforts to reform its cannabis laws most notably through citizen-led ballot initiatives. Advocates for medical cannabis have collected enough signatures to place initiatives on the ballot but these efforts have faced significant legal challenges from state officials who argue that cannabis reform initiatives violate Nebraska's constitution.

The fight for cannabis reform in Nebraska is being led by grassroots organizations patients and advocates who believe that cannabis could provide much-needed relief for those suffering from conditions like chronic pain epilepsy PTSD and cancer. Despite the challenges they face advocates are determined to bring medical cannabis to the state and are working tirelessly to educate the public and push for change.

The resistance to cannabis reform in Nebraska is largely driven by conservative lawmakers and law enforcement agencies who argue that cannabis poses a threat to public safety and could lead to increased crime and drug use. This opposition has made it difficult for reform efforts to gain traction in the state even as public opinion shifts in favor of legalization.

However there is growing hope that Nebraska will eventually embrace cannabis reform. As more states across the Midwest move toward legalization there is increasing pressure on Nebraska lawmakers to reconsider their stance on cannabis. With neighboring states like South Dakota and Missouri adopting medical cannabis programs Nebraska may soon find itself surrounded by states with legal cannabis markets Advocates are hopeful that this regional momentum will lead to a shift in Nebraska's cannabis policies.

Chapter 35 South Dakota A Legal Rollercoaster for Cannabis

South Dakota has had a tumultuous relationship with cannabis reform In 2020 the state made headlines by becoming the first in the nation to pass both medical and recreational cannabis legalization measures in the same election. However the path to legalization has been anything but smooth with legal challenges and political opposition stalling the implementation of these laws.

The 2020 election was a historic moment for cannabis reform in South Dakota Voters approved both Initiated Measure 26 which established a medical cannabis program and Amendment A which legalized recreational cannabis for adults over the age of 21. These measures were seen as a major victory for cannabis advocates who had long pushed for reform in the deeply conservative state.

However shortly after the election South Dakota's governor and law enforcement agencies filed a lawsuit challenging the constitutionality of Amendment A. The state's Supreme Court ultimately struck down the recreational cannabis measure ruling that it violated the state's single subject rule for ballot initiatives. This decision effectively halted the implementation of recreational cannabis in South Dakota leaving the state in legal limbo.

Despite the setback the state's medical cannabis program has moved forward with patients now able to access medical cannabis for a variety of qualifying conditions including chronic pain epilepsy and cancer The South Dakota Department of Health oversees the program and has begun issuing medical cannabis cards to eligible patients while licensed dispensaries have started opening across the state

The legal challenges surrounding cannabis reform in South Dakota have created uncertainty for both patients and businesses Advocates are hopeful that the state will eventually move toward full legalization particularly as public support for cannabis reform continues to grow South Dakota's experience serves as a reminder of the complex legal and political landscape surrounding cannabis reform in the United States

Chapter 36 North Dakota Medical Marijuana in the Prairie State

North Dakota is another conservative state that has taken cautious steps toward cannabis reform In 2016 voters approved Measure 5 which established a medical marijuana program in the state allowing patients with certain qualifying conditions to access cannabis for therapeutic purposes. Since then the state has made gradual progress in expanding access to medical cannabis though recreational cannabis remains illegal.

North Dakota's medical marijuana program is regulated by the North Dakota Department of Health which oversees the licensing of dispensaries cultivators and processors. Patients with conditions such as chronic pain epilepsy cancer and PTSD are eligible to apply for a medical marijuana card and can purchase cannabis products from licensed dispensaries across the state

Despite the success of the state's medical marijuana program efforts to legalize recreational cannabis have been met with resistance In 2018 North Dakota voters rejected a ballot initiative that would have legalized recreational cannabis for adults over the age of 21. This was a setback for cannabis advocates who had hoped to follow in the footsteps of other states that had embraced full legalization. However there is still strong support for cannabis reform in North Dakota and advocates continue to push for change

One of the challenges facing cannabis reform in North Dakota is the state's conservative political landscape. Many lawmakers remain opposed to both medical and recreational cannabis arguing that legalization could lead to negative social and public safety consequences. Despite these concerns public support for cannabis reform has been steadily increasing particularly as more states across the country legalize both medical and recreational cannabis.

The Future of Cannabis Reform in North Dakota

The future of cannabis reform in North Dakota will depend on continued advocacy efforts and changes in public opinion. While the state's medical marijuana program has been a success there is still significant opposition to the idea of full recreational cannabis legalization. However as more states across the Midwest move toward legalization there is increasing pressure on North Dakota lawmakers to reconsider their stance on cannabis

Advocates are hopeful that North Dakota will eventually join the growing number of states that have embraced both medical and recreational cannabis legalization. If North Dakota fully embraces cannabis reform it could not only improve patient access to therapeutic cannabis products but also create significant economic opportunities for the state

was seen as a significant setback for advocates pushing for broader cannabis reform in the state. Despite this, advocates continue to push for legalization, citing the growing demand for cannabis reform both within North Dakota and nationwide.

Chapter 37: Montana - Expanding Access in Big Sky Country

Montana, often known for its wide-open spaces and rugged landscapes, has been making strides in cannabis reform, particularly with the legalization of recreational cannabis in 2020. The state's earlier adoption of medical marijuana in 2004 paved the way for broader reforms, with strong public support behind the move to expand cannabis access. Today, Montana's cannabis industry is rapidly growing, with both medical and recreational users able to access cannabis products from licensed dispensaries.

Montana's Medical Marijuana Program and Legalization of Recreational Use

Montana has had a medical marijuana program in place for nearly two decades, but the state's cannabis industry truly expanded in 2020 when voters approved Initiative 190, which legalized recreational cannabis for adults over the age of 21. The passage of Initiative 190 marked a major turning point for cannabis reform in Montana, creating a legal framework for the cultivation, sale, and possession of cannabis for recreational use.

Under Montana's recreational cannabis laws, adults are allowed to possess up to one ounce of cannabis or eight grams of concentrates. Residents are also permitted to grow up to four cannabis plants for personal use, provided they adhere to the state's regulations on cultivation.

The Dispensary Scene in Montana

Montana's cannabis dispensaries have flourished since the legalization of recreational cannabis, with licensed businesses opening across the state to serve both medical and recreational users. Billings, the largest city in Montana, has become a hub for the state's cannabis industry, with dispensaries offering a variety of cannabis products to meet the needs of both medical patients and adult consumers.

Cannabis Tourism in Montana

Montana's scenic beauty and outdoor recreation opportunities make it a prime destination for cannabis tourism, particularly as the state's recreational cannabis market continues to grow. Tourists visiting cities like Billings, Missoula, and Bozeman can explore Montana's dispensaries and experience the state's unique approach to cannabis, while also enjoying the breathtaking landscapes that the state is known for.

In addition to its urban attractions, Montana's outdoor recreational opportunities, such as hiking, skiing, and fishing, make it an ideal location for cannabis-friendly tourism. Tourists can enjoy the state's natural beauty while partaking in legal cannabis, making Montana one of the most exciting new destinations for cannabis enthusiasts.

Chapter 38: Wyoming - A Slow Embrace of Cannabis Reform

Wyoming, one of the most conservative states in the U.S., has been slow to embrace cannabis reform compared to its neighbors. Both medical marijuana and recreational cannabis remain illegal in Wyoming, and the state enforces strict penalties for cannabis possession. However, public opinion is shifting, and there is growing momentum among residents and advocates for the legalization of medical cannabis.

The Role of Hemp and CBD in Wyoming's Cannabis Market

Wyoming's cannabis industry is primarily centered around hemp cultivation and CBD products, which are legal under federal law as long as they meet the 0.3% THC threshold. The state's hemp industry has grown slowly since the legalization of industrial hemp, with Wyoming farmers beginning to cultivate hemp for CBD extraction and other uses. While hemp farming remains a small part of Wyoming's agricultural economy, there is potential for growth as demand for CBD products continues to increase.

Cannabis Advocacy in Wyoming

Despite Wyoming's conservative stance on cannabis, there is a growing movement among residents and advocates to push for cannabis reform, particularly the legalization of medical marijuana. Advocacy groups like Wyoming NORML (National Organization for the Reform of Marijuana Laws) have been at the forefront of efforts to educate lawmakers and the public about the benefits of medical cannabis.

Advocates argue that patients with debilitating conditions, such as chronic pain, epilepsy, PTSD, and cancer, deserve access to medical cannabis as a safe and effective treatment option. Currently, Wyoming does not allow for the use of medical marijuana, but advocates continue to push for legislation that would expand access to cannabis for patients in need.

Chapter 39: Minnesota - Medical Marijuana and Potential for Growth

Minnesota is one of the states that has embraced medical marijuana, but the state's medical cannabis program is more restrictive than many others in the U.S. While medical marijuana has been legal in Minnesota since 2014, the state prohibits the sale of smokable cannabis, allowing only tinctures, capsules, topicals, and vape products. Despite these limitations, Minnesota's medical marijuana market continues to grow, with patients gaining access to a wider range of cannabis products in recent years.

The cities of Minneapolis and St. Paul have become focal points for the state's cannabis industry, with medical dispensaries and cannabis-friendly wellness centers offering therapeutic cannabis products to patients. Minnesota's medical cannabis program has proven to be effective for patients with conditions like chronic pain, epilepsy, cancer, and PTSD, and advocates are pushing for further reforms that would expand access to cannabis for more residents.

The Dispensary Scene in Minnesota

While Minnesota's medical marijuana program prohibits the sale of smokable flower, the state's dispensaries offer a variety of cannabis products, including tinctures, vape, cartridges, and edibles. Dispensaries are concentrated in urban areas like Minneapolis and St. Paul, where patients can access medical cannabis with a recommendation from a licensed physician.

Minnesota's medical cannabis dispensaries are heavily regulated, with a focus on patient safety and product quality. These dispensaries provide patients with education and guidance on how to use cannabis effectively for their medical conditions, ensuring that patients can make informed decisions about their cannabis therapy.

Chapter 40: New Mexico - Cannabis and the Land of Enchantment

New Mexico, often referred to as the Land of Enchantment, has a long history of progressive policies regarding cannabis use. The state's unique cultural blend, shaped by Indigenous, Hispanic, and Anglo influences, has played a significant role in its evolving cannabis culture. In 2007, New Mexico became one of the earliest states to legalize medical cannabis through the Lynn and Erin Compassionate Use Act, and in 2021, New Mexico took the bold step of legalizing recreational cannabis, cementing its place as a leader in cannabis reform.

New Mexico's cannabis culture reflects the state's broader emphasis on wellness, creativity, and natural healing. The state's scenic landscapes, from the high desert to the Sangre de Cristo Mountains, provide the perfect backdrop for a growing cannabis tourism industry, with dispensaries, cannabis-friendly events, and wellness retreats attracting visitors from around the country.

The Passage of Recreational Cannabis in New Mexico

The legalization of recreational cannabis in New Mexico came in 2021 with the passage of the Cannabis Regulation Act, which allows adults over the age of 21 to purchase and possess up to two ounces of cannabis. This landmark legislation marked a major turning point for New Mexico's cannabis culture, transforming the state from a pioneer in medical cannabis to a leader in the adult-use market. The state's medical cannabis program, which has been in place for over a decade, has provided a strong foundation for the development of the recreational cannabis industry.

Cannabis Culture in New Mexico's Major Cities

Santa Fe, the capital of New Mexico, is known for its rich history, vibrant arts scene, and commitment to holistic health. The city's cannabis culture is deeply intertwined with its focus on wellness, with numerous dispensaries and wellness centers offering cannabis-based therapies for conditions like chronic pain, anxiety, and PTSD. Santa Fe's residents and visitors alike are embracing cannabis as a natural part of their health and wellness routines, making the city a key destination for cannabis tourism in New Mexico.

Albuquerque, New Mexico's largest city, has also embraced the state's cannabis movement, with a growing number of dispensaries and cannabis-friendly businesses catering to the city's diverse population. Albuquerque's cannabis culture is closely tied to its thriving music, art, and food scenes, with local businesses incorporating cannabis into their offerings. From CBD-infused meals to cannabis-themed art events, Albuquerque is at the forefront of New Mexico's evolving cannabis industry.

Taos, a small town known for its stunning landscapes and strong Indigenous influences, has become a haven for cannabis enthusiasts seeking relaxation and creativity. Taos' emphasis on sustainability and natural health has made it a focal point for New Mexico's cannabis culture, with cannabis-friendly wellness retreats, hemp farms, and dispensaries contributing to the town's laid-back, bohemian vibe.

Cannabis Tourism in New Mexico

New Mexico's unique combination of natural beauty, cultural diversity, and progressive cannabis policies has made it a prime destination for cannabis tourism. Visitors to the state can explore dispensaries, cannabis-friendly events, and wellness retreats while taking in the stunning landscapes of the Southwest.

In cities like Santa Fe and Taos, tourists can enjoy CBD-infused spa treatments, hemp-friendly yoga classes, and cannabis-themed tours that highlight the state's rich history and artistic heritage. Albuquerque offers a more urban experience, with dispensaries, cannabis-friendly cafes, and CBD shops providing visitors with access to a wide range of cannabis products.

Chapter 41: Utah - A Conservative Approach to Medical Cannabis

Utah, known for its deeply conservative values and large Latter-day Saint (LDS) population, has taken a cautious and highly regulated approach to medical cannabis. Despite its conservative reputation, Utah became one of the many states to legalize medical cannabis in 2018 through Proposition 2, signaling a shift in public opinion toward the therapeutic benefits of cannabis. However, Utah's cannabis laws remain some of the most restrictive in the country, reflecting the state's emphasis on medical use over recreational consumption.

Utah's cannabis culture is still in its infancy, but the state's medical cannabis program is providing relief to patients suffering from conditions like chronic pain, epilepsy, and cancer. Cities like Salt Lake City and Provo are home to a growing number of dispensaries and wellness centers, where patients can access cannabis products that meet the state's strict regulatory requirements.

The Passage of Proposition 2 and Medical Cannabis in Utah

In 2018, Utah voters approved Proposition 2, a ballot measure that legalized medical cannabis for patients with qualifying conditions. The passage of Proposition 2 marked a significant victory for cannabis advocates in Utah, as the state's conservative political climate had long resisted any form of cannabis legalization. However, following the passage of Proposition 2, the Utah State Legislature made several amendments to the law, creating a highly regulated and restrictive medical cannabis program.

Cannabis Culture in Utah's Major Cities

Utah's cannabis culture is still in its early stages, but cities like Salt Lake City and Provo are beginning to embrace the state's medical cannabis program. Salt Lake City, the state's capital, is home to several medical cannabis pharmacies that provide patients with access to cannabis-based therapies for a variety of conditions. Salt Lake City's residents are increasingly turning to cannabis as a natural alternative to prescription medications, particularly for conditions like chronic pain and anxiety.

In Provo, a city known for its conservative values and large LDS population, cannabis is still viewed with some skepticism, but the success of Utah's medical cannabis program has helped shift public opinion. Dispensaries in Provo offer a limited selection of medical cannabis products, and local patients are beginning to see the benefits of cannabis for chronic health conditions.

Chapter 42: Idaho - Resistance to Cannabis in the Gem State

Idaho, known as the Gem State, stands as one of the few remaining U.S. states where cannabis reform has made little progress. Unlike many of its neighboring states, which have embraced medical and recreational cannabis, Idaho has resisted calls for legalization and continues to enforce some of the strictest cannabis laws in the country. Both medical marijuana and recreational cannabis remains illegal in Idaho, and the state has shown little interest in changing its approach to cannabis policy.

Despite Idaho's strict cannabis laws, there is a growing movement among residents and advocates to push for medical cannabis legalization, particularly as neighboring states like Montana and Oregon have seen success with their cannabis programs. However, Idaho's cannabis culture remains largely underground, with most residents relying on CBD products and hemp-derived remedies for relief from conditions like anxiety and chronic pain.

The Fight for Cannabis Reform in Idaho

Idaho's conservative political climate has made it one of the most resistant states to cannabis reform, with state lawmakers consistently opposing efforts to legalize medical marijuana or decriminalize cannabis possession. Advocacy groups like Idaho NORML have worked tirelessly to push for medical cannabis legislation, but they have faced significant opposition from both the state legislature and conservative residents.

One of the key issues in Idaho's cannabis debate is the influence of the Idaho State Constitution, which explicitly prohibits the legalization of controlled substances like cannabis. As a result, any effort to legalize medical cannabis or create a recreational market would require a constitutional amendment, a challenging prospect given the state's political landscape.

While the state's cannabis laws remain restrictive, the increasing availability of CBD products is helping to normalize cannabis use for some Idahoans, especially those interested in wellness and holistic health. Cities like Boise are becoming focal points for this emerging CBD culture, where local businesses are incorporating hemp-derived products into their offerings and advocating for the benefits of natural health remedies.

At the same time, cannabis advocacy groups in Idaho continue to push for broader reform, including the legalization of medical marijuana. While progress has been slow, advocates remain hopeful that growing public support for cannabis reform will eventually lead to changes in state law, allowing patients in Idaho access to medical cannabis for therapeutic use. For now, the CBD market in Idaho is providing residents with a glimpse into the potential benefits of cannabis-derived products, even as the debate over full legalization continues.

The future of cannabis in Idaho may remain uncertain, but with the steady growth of the hemp industry and increasing awareness of CBD's therapeutic potential, advocates are optimistic that change is on the horizon.

Chapter 43: Alaska - Pioneering Cannabis in the Last Frontier

Alaska is one of the most unique states when it comes to cannabis reform. Known for its vast wilderness, long winters, and remote communities, Alaska has a rich history of progressive cannabis policies that distinguish it from many other states. As early as 1975, Alaska decriminalized possession of small amounts of cannabis, and the state has since continued to blaze a trail in the world of cannabis legalization. In 2014, Alaska became one of the first states to legalize recreational cannabis, allowing adults over the age of 21 to possess, grow, and purchase cannabis.

With legal dispensaries now operating in cities like Anchorage, Juneau, and Fairbanks, Alaska's cannabis industry has become a significant part of the state's economy. The state's recreational cannabis market is thriving, attracting both locals and tourists who are interested in experiencing the unique cannabis culture of the Last Frontier.

Alaska's Early Adoption of Cannabis Reform

Alaska's relationship with cannabis dates back to 1975, when the state's Supreme Court ruled in Ravin v. State that adults could possess small amounts of cannabis for personal use in their homes. This ruling effectively decriminalized cannabis in the state, making Alaska one of the most progressive states in the U.S. when it came to cannabis policy. Despite attempts by the federal government and state lawmakers to roll back cannabis protections in the 1980s and 1990s, Alaska maintained its reputation as a trailblazer in cannabis reform.

In 1998, Alaska voters approved Ballot Measure 8, which established a medical marijuana program for patients with qualifying conditions such as cancer, chronic pain, and HIV/AIDS. This program allowed patients to legally possess and cultivate cannabis for personal use, though it did not create a framework for dispensaries. The passage of Ballot Measure 8 further cemented Alaska's role as a leader in cannabis reform.

Recreational Cannabis Legalization in Alaska

In 2014, Alaska voters approved Ballot Measure 2, which legalized the recreational use of cannabis for adults over the age of 21. The law allows adults to possess up to one ounce of cannabis, grow up to six plants, and purchase cannabis from licensed dispensaries. The state's cannabis industry officially launched in 2016, with the opening of the first recreational dispensaries.

Alaska's recreational cannabis market is unique in that it serves both local residents and tourists who visit the state to experience its stunning natural beauty and vibrant cannabis culture. Dispensaries in cities like Anchorage, Fairbanks, and Juneau offer a wide range of cannabis products, including flower, edibles, tinctures, and concentrates. These dispensaries cater to a diverse clientele, from residents looking for therapeutic relief to tourists eager to explore the Alaskan wilderness while enjoying cannabis.

Cannabis Tourism in Alaska

Alaska's cannabis tourism industry has grown steadily since the legalization of recreational cannabis. Visitors to cities like Anchorage and Juneau can enjoy cannabis-friendly tours, explore local dispensaries, and experience the state's stunning landscapes while partaking in legal cannabis. The state's cannabis culture is deeply intertwined with its emphasis on the outdoors, making it an ideal destination for tourists looking to combine cannabis with activities like hiking, fishing, and wildlife watching.

In addition to the recreational cannabis market, Alaska is home to a number of hemp farms and CBD businesses that cater to visitors interested in the therapeutic benefits of hemp-derived products. Tourists can explore hemp farms, visit CBD shops, and participate in wellness retreats that promote the use of cannabis and hemp products for health and relaxation.

Challenges and Opportunities in Alaska's Cannabis Industry

Despite the success of Alaska's recreational cannabis market, the state faces several challenges, particularly in terms of regulation and distribution. Alaska's vast size and remote communities make it difficult for dispensaries to serve the entire state, and many residents in rural areas have limited access to cannabis products. Additionally, the state's harsh climate and long winters present challenges for cannabis cultivation, as growers must rely on indoor facilities to produce high-quality cannabis year-round.

However, despite these challenges, Alaska's cannabis industry offers significant opportunities for growth, particularly in areas like tourism, cannabis cultivation, and product development. As demand for cannabis products continues to grow, Alaska's cannabis businesses are well-positioned to thrive, particularly in the state's larger cities and popular tourist destinations.

Chapter 44: Delaware - A Small State with Big Steps in Cannabis Reform

Delaware, one of the smallest states in the U.S., has made significant progress in cannabis reform over the past decade. In 2011, Delaware became the 16th state to legalize medical marijuana, and in 2015, the state decriminalized the possession of small amounts of cannabis. While recreational cannabis remains illegal in Delaware, the state's medical marijuana program is expanding rapidly, providing patients with access to cannabis products for a variety of medical conditions.

Delaware's Medical Marijuana Program

Delaware's medical marijuana program was established in 2011 with the passage of Senate Bill 17, also known as the Delaware Medical Marijuana Act. The law allows patients with qualifying conditions, such as cancer, chronic pain, HIV/AIDS, and PTSD, to obtain a medical marijuana car, which allows them to purchase cannabis products from state-licensed dispensaries.

The program is overseen by the Delaware Department of Health and Social Services (DHSS), which is responsible for regulating the cultivation, production, and distribution of medical cannabis. Since its inception, Delaware's medical marijuana program has grown steadily, with dispensaries opening in cities like Wilmington, Dover, and Newark.

Chapter 45: Maryland - The Growth of Medical Cannabis in the Mid-Atlantic

Maryland has emerged as a leader in the medical cannabis industry, with one of the most successful medical marijuana programs in the country. Since the legalization of medical cannabis in 2014, Maryland's cannabis market has grown rapidly, with dispensaries opening in cities across the state, including Baltimore, Silver Spring, and Columbia.

Maryland's medical marijuana program is considered one of the most comprehensive in the U.S., allowing patients with a wide range of medical conditions to access cannabis products for therapeutic use. The state's cannabis industry is expanding rapidly, providing economic opportunities and improving patient access to medical cannabis.

Maryland's medical marijuana program is considered one of the most comprehensive in the U.S., allowing patients with a wide range of medical conditions to access cannabis products for therapeutic use. The state's cannabis industry is expanding rapidly, providing economic opportunities and improving patient access to medical cannabis. Since the program's launch in 2017, Maryland has seen significant growth in both dispensaries and cannabis production facilities, helping to meet the needs of its growing patient population.

Cities like Baltimore, Annapolis, and Columbia are home to many of the state's medical cannabis dispensaries, offering a variety of cannabis-based therapies, from flower to edibles, topicals, and concentrates. Maryland's cannabis community continues to advocate for better patient access and is pushing for recreational legalization, with strong public support building momentum for broader reform.

The Evolution of Maryland's Medical Marijuana Program

Maryland's medical marijuana program was established through legislation passed in 2014, but it wasn't until 2017 that the program fully launched and dispensaries began serving patients. The program allows patients with qualifying medical conditions, such as chronic pain, PTSD, epilepsy, and multiple sclerosis, to obtain a medical marijuana card and purchase cannabis products from licensed dispensaries across the state. The state's program has grown rapidly, with tens of thousands of patients now enrolled and regularly accessing medical cannabis for therapeutic use.

The Maryland Medical Cannabis Commission (MMCC) oversees the program, ensuring that both patients and businesses comply with state regulations. The MMCC is responsible for licensing cultivators, processors, and dispensaries, and it plays a key role in maintaining product safety standards and ensuring that cannabis products meet rigorous quality controls.

One of the unique aspects of Maryland's program is the variety of cannabis products available to patients. Dispensaries offer flower, concentrates, tinctures, capsules, and edibles, giving patients numerous options to find the best form of cannabis therapy for their specific needs. Additionally, Maryland's medical cannabis program places a strong emphasis on patient education, with dispensaries providing information about the therapeutic uses of cannabis and how to consume it safely.

The Dispensary Scene in Maryland

Maryland's dispensary scene is thriving, with licensed dispensaries operating in cities across the state. Baltimore, the largest city in Maryland, has become a hub for the state's medical cannabis industry, offering patients access to a wide range of cannabis products. Baltimore's dispensaries cater to patients with various conditions, providing personalized care and guidance on how to incorporate medical cannabis into their treatment plans.

In Annapolis, the state's capital, dispensaries are known for their emphasis on patient education and cannabis wellness. Patients in Annapolis can access a wide selection of cannabis-based therapies, with dispensaries offering detailed information on the benefits of medical cannabis for conditions like anxiety, depression, and chronic pain. The city's cannabis community is closely tied to its wellness culture, with dispensaries playing a key role in promoting the therapeutic potential of cannabis.

Columbia, located between Baltimore and Washington D.C., is another key player in Maryland's medical marijuana market. Dispensaries in Columbia offer patients access to a diverse range of cannabis products, from edibles and tinctures to flower and vape cartridges. The city's cannabis culture is deeply rooted in its focus on health and well-being, with many residents turning to medical cannabis as a natural alternative to traditional pharmaceuticals.

Cannabis Advocacy in Maryland

Maryland's cannabis reform movement has been largely driven by patients, advocates, and organizations working to expand access to medical cannabis and push for the legalization of recreational cannabis. Groups like Maryland NORML (National Organization for the Reform of Marijuana Laws) and the Maryland Cannabis Policy Coalition played a key role in advocating for the passage of the state's medical marijuana law, and they continue to push for broader cannabis reform.

Advocates in Maryland argue that the state's successful medical cannabis program demonstrates that Maryland is ready for recreational legalization. Recent polling shows that a majority of Maryland residents support the legalization of recreational cannabis, and there is growing pressure on lawmakers to pass legislation that would allow adults over the age of 21 to purchase and use cannabis for personal use.

In addition to pushing for recreational legalization, advocates are working to improve the state's medical cannabis program by expanding patient access and addressing affordability concerns. Many patients, particularly those in rural areas, still face challenges in accessing medical cannabis, and the cost of cannabis products can be prohibitive for some. Advocacy groups are calling for reforms that would lower the price of cannabis products and ensure that dispensaries are accessible to patients across the state.

Cannabis Culture in Maryland's Major Cities

Maryland's cannabis culture is thriving, particularly in cities like Baltimore, Annapolis, and Columbia, where medical marijuana dispensaries and cannabis-friendly events are becoming more common. These cities are home to vibrant cannabis communities, with local businesses, patients, and advocates working together to promote the therapeutic benefits of cannabis and push for broader cannabis reform.

Baltimore, with its rich history and diverse population, has embraced the medical cannabis industry, with dispensaries and wellness centers offering patients access to a variety of cannabis-based therapies. The city's cannabis culture is closely tied to its focus on community health and well-being, and Baltimore's residents have been at the forefront of efforts to expand access to medical cannabis.

Annapolis, known for its historic charm and waterfront views, has also embraced the medical cannabis market. The city's dispensaries cater to patients seeking relief from conditions like chronic pain, anxiety, and PTSD, and local businesses have incorporated CBD and hemp-based products into their wellness offerings. Annapolis' cannabis culture is closely aligned with its emphasis on health and wellness, making it a key player in Maryland's cannabis reform movement.

In Columbia, home to a diverse and progressive community, cannabis culture is thriving as more residents turn to medical marijuana for therapeutic purposes. The city's dispensaries provide patients with access to cannabis-based therapies, and Columbia's progressive attitudes have made it a focal point for efforts to expand access to medical cannabis and push for recreational legalization.

Cannabis Tourism in Maryland

While recreational cannabis is not yet legal in Maryland, the state's medical marijuana program and CBD industry are attracting visitors interested in wellness tourism and cannabis-based therapies. Cities like Baltimore and Annapolis offer tourists access to medical cannabis dispensaries, CBD shops, and wellness centers, providing a unique way for visitors to experience Maryland's emerging cannabis culture.

Baltimore, known for its arts scene and historical landmarks, is a popular destination for cannabis tourists seeking medical cannabis or CBD-infused products. Visitors to Baltimore can explore the city's dispensaries and wellness centers, which offer a variety of cannabis-based therapies for patients and consumers.

Annapolis, with its scenic waterfront and vibrant downtown, is another key destination for cannabis tourism. Tourists visiting Annapolis can explore the city's growing cannabis industry, including dispensaries, CBD shops, and hemp-friendly wellness centers. Annapolis' cannabis culture is deeply intertwined with its focus on health and wellness, making it an ideal destination for those interested in learning more about the therapeutic benefits of cannabis.

Cannabis Festivals and Events in Maryland

Maryland is home to a growing number of cannabis-themed festivals, expos, and educational events that celebrate the state's evolving cannabis market. One of the most notable events is the Maryland Cannabis Expo, which brings together patients, advocates, and industry professionals to discuss the latest developments in the medical cannabis industry and explore the future of cannabis reform in Maryland.

Another popular event is the Mid-Atlantic Cannabis Conference, which focuses on the potential of the cannabis industry in Maryland and the broader Mid-Atlantic region. The conference features educational panels, product showcases, and networking opportunities for those involved in the cannabis industry.

In addition to these larger events, Maryland is home to a growing number of cannabis-friendly pop-up markets, wellness retreats, and educational workshops that promote the health benefits of cannabis. These events provide consumers with an opportunity to learn more about the therapeutic uses of cannabis and connect with local cannabis businesses.

Chapter 46: Connecticut - The Future of Cannabis on the East Coast

Connecticut, like many states in the Northeast, is embracing cannabis reform, particularly with the recent legalization of recreational cannabis in 2021. This step has made Connecticut a key player in the evolving East Coast cannabis market, and the state is positioning itself as a hub for both medical and recreational cannabis. As Connecticut builds out its legal cannabis framework, cities like Hartford,New Haven, and Bridgeport are becoming focal points of the state's emerging cannabis culture.

The Passage of Recreational Cannabis Legalization

The legalization of adult-use cannabis in Connecticut represents a significant shift in the state's approach to cannabis reform. The law allows adults over the age of 21 to purchase and possess up to 1.5 ounces of cannabis for personal use, while home cultivation is set to become legal for adults by 2023. The law also creates a framework for cannabis retail businesses, including dispensaries, cultivators, and manufacturers, to obtain licenses and operate in a highly regulated market.

Cannabis Culture in Connecticut's Major Cities

As Connecticut rolls out its recreational cannabis program, cities like Hartford, New Haven, and Bridgeport are leading the charge in developing a rich cannabis culture that combines wellness, community engagement, and entrepreneurship.

Hartford, the state capital, is rapidly becoming a center for cannabis events, dispensaries, and wellness retreats. The city's progressive attitudes toward cannabis have made it a hub for advocates and consumers seeking cannabis-based health products and services. Hartford's cannabis culture is rooted in its community-centered approach, with local businesses offering CBD-infused treatments, cannabis-themed events, and workshops focused on responsible consumption and wellness.

In New Haven, home to Yale University, the focus is on fostering a cannabis-friendly environment that blends with the city's intellectual and cultural life. The city's cafes, wellness centers, and local events have embraced CBD products and are preparing for the state's growing adult-use market. New Haven's cannabis scene thrives on its connection to innovation and research, with local entrepreneurs and academics working together to push the boundaries of cannabis products and their applications in health and wellness.

Bridgeport, Connecticut's largest city, is also seeing a surge in cannabis-related businesses. With a rich history of industry and commerce, Bridgeport is attracting a wave of cannabis entrepreneurs looking to open dispensaries and cannabis lounges that cater to both medical patients and recreational consumers. The city's cannabis culture is growing alongside its diverse community, with a focus on inclusion, education, and promoting social equity within the cannabis industry.

Cannabis Tourism in Connecticut

As Connecticut's cannabis market continues to grow, the state is positioning itself as a potential destination for cannabis tourism. With its proximity to major cities like New York and Boston, Connecticut is an attractive spot for cannabis-friendly events, wellness retreats, and dispensary tours. Visitors to cities like Hartford and New Haven can expect to find cannabis-themed experiences ranging from CBD spa treatments to cannabis culinary classes, making the state a key destination for East Coast cannabis tourism.

Chapter 47: Rhode Island - Small State, Big Cannabis Reforms

Though Rhode Island may be the smallest state in the U.S., it is making significant strides in cannabis reform, particularly with the legalization of medical marijuana and the growing push for recreational cannabis. Rhode Island's cannabis culture is emerging quickly, and cities like Providence are playing a central role in shaping the state's approach to cannabis legalization.

Cannabis Legalization Efforts in Rhode Island

Rhode Island first legalized medical marijuana in 2006, becoming one of the early adopters of medical cannabis on the East Coast. The state has since expanded access to medical marijuana, allowing patients with conditions such as chronic pain, cancer, and PTSD to access cannabis through a network of licensed dispensaries. With the success of the medical cannabis program, there has been increasing momentum toward recreational cannabis legalization, with advocates and lawmakers working to pass legislation that would allow for adult-use sales.

Cannabis Culture in Providence

Providence, Rhode Island's capital and largest city, is at the heart of the state's cannabis culture. Known for its thriving arts scene and progressive values, Providence has embraced the cannabis industry as part of its broader push toward wellness and community-driven business. The city is home to several medical cannabis dispensaries that serve patients from across the state, and these dispensaries are helping to normalize cannabis use while promoting education and responsible consumption.

Providence's cannabis culture extends beyond dispensaries, with a growing number of cannabis-friendly events and CBD shops offering products designed to enhance both physical and mental well-being. The city's restaurants and cafes are also starting to experiment with CBD-infused dishes and drinks, providing locals and visitors with a unique way to explore cannabis as part of the culinary experience.

Cannabis Festivals and Events in Rhode Island

Rhode Island is home to a growing number of cannabis-related events, particularly in Providence. The city hosts cannabis expos,educational panels, and wellness retreats that bring together patients, advocates, and industry professionals to discuss the latest developments in the state's cannabis market. Events like the Rhode Island Cannabis Convention have helped to elevate the state's cannabis industry by providing a platform for local businesses to showcase their products and services while also promoting cannabis advocacy and education.

Chapter 48: Maine - A Hub for Craft Cannabis in the Northeast

Maine has emerged as a leader in cannabis reform in the Northeast, with the state being one of the earliest to legalize recreational cannabis in 2016. Known for its emphasis on small businesses and craft culture, Maine's approach to cannabis has focused on creating a market that supports local growers, artisanal cannabis products, and community-driven dispensaries. Cities like Portland and Bangor are at the center of Maine's thriving cannabis industry, with a focus on sustainability, quality, and craftsmanship.

The Craft Cannabis Scene in Maine

Maine's craft cannabis industry is one of the most respected in the U.S., with a reputation for producing high-quality cannabis that reflects the state's commitment to supporting local farmers and small-scale cultivation. The state's cannabis laws are designed to prioritize Maine-based businesses, making it an ideal location for craft cannabis entrepreneurs who value sustainability and artisanal production methods.

Portland, the state's largest city, is a hub for craft cannabis. The city is home to a growing number of boutique dispensaries that offer a curated selection of locally grown cannabis, edibles, concentrates, and topicals. Portland's cannabis culture is closely tied to its focus on local businesses and sustainability, with many dispensaries emphasizing organic growing practices and environmentally friendly packaging.

In Bangor, located in central Maine, the focus is on creating a community-driven cannabis market that supports local growers and cultivators. Dispensaries in Bangor are known for offering craft cannabis strains that cater to both medical patients and recreational consumers, with a focus on promoting education and responsible consumption.

Cannabis Tourism in Maine

Maine's reputation as a hub for craft cannabis has made it a popular destination for cannabis tourists looking to experience the state's unique approach to cannabis culture. Visitors to cities like Portland and Bangor can explore cannabis-friendly wellness retreats, dispensary tours, and CBD-infused culinary experiences. Maine's focus on local craftsmanship and sustainability extends to its cannabis industry, making it an ideal destination for tourists seeking high-quality, artisanal cannabis.

In addition to its urban attractions, Maine's natural beauty also makes it an appealing location for cannabis-friendly outdoor experiences, such as CBD-infused spa treatments and cannabis-friendly hiking tours. With its blend of craft culture and outdoor recreation, Maine is positioned to be a leader in the cannabis tourism market.

Chapter 49: West Virginia - Medical Cannabis in the Mountain State

West Virginia, often known for its rugged natural beauty and rich cultural heritage, has recently joined the ranks of states that have legalized medical cannabis. Despite its historically conservative stance on cannabis, the passage of the Medical Cannabis Act in 2017 marked a significant step forward for cannabis reform in the Mountain State. This legislation allows patients with specific qualifying conditions to access medical cannabis under strict regulatory guidelines. While recreational cannabis remains illegal, West Virginia's medical cannabis program is gaining momentum, offering new economic opportunities and expanding access to therapeutic cannabis products for residents.

The Medical Cannabis Act and Its Implementation

The passage of the Medical Cannabis Act in 2017 established a legal framework for medical marijuana in West Virginia. Under this legislation, patients with qualifying conditions such as chronic pain, PTSD, epilepsy, HIV/AIDS, multiple sclerosis, and cancer can apply for a medical cannabis card with a physician's recommendation. The law allows for the production and sale of medical cannabis products, including oils, tinctures, pills, topicals, and vape products. However, smokable flower remains prohibited under the current legal framework.

The West Virginia Office of Medical Cannabis (OMC) oversees the licensing of dispensaries, cultivators, and processors, ensuring that medical cannabis products meet strict safety and quality standards. Since the program's implementation, a growing number of dispensaries have opened across the state, offering medical cannabis to patients in need.

Despite initial challenges in rolling out the program, such as delays in issuing licenses and opening dispensaries, West Virginia's medical cannabis program is steadily expanding. Advocates continue to push for improvements in patient access, particularly in rural areas where dispensaries may be scarce.

The Dispensary Scene in West Virginia

West Virginia's medical cannabis market is still in its early stages, with dispensaries gradually opening across the state. Charleston, the state capital, and cities like Huntington and Morgantown are home to some of the first medical cannabis dispensaries in West Virginia, offering patients access to a variety of cannabis-based therapies.

Charleston, as the political and cultural center of the state, has become a hub for medical cannabis patients seeking relief from debilitating conditions. Dispensaries in Charleston provide patients with access to high-quality cannabis products, including tinctures, topicals, and vape cartridges, all tailored to meet the specific needs of medical cannabis users.

In Morgantown, home to West Virginia University, dispensaries cater to both students and local residents seeking medical cannabis treatments. The city's progressive attitudes toward cannabis reform make Morgantown an important location for the state's medical marijuana program, and local businesses are actively participating in efforts to expand patient access to cannabis.

Cannabis Advocacy in West Virginia

West Virginia's cannabis reform movement has been driven by a coalition of patients, advocates, and physicians who recognize the therapeutic benefits of cannabis. Organizations like West Virginia NORML (National Organization for the Reform of Marijuana Laws) and WV for Medical Cannabis have played key roles in advocating for the passage of the Medical Cannabis Act and continue to push for improvements to the state's medical cannabis program.

Advocates are calling for the legalization of smokable flower and the expansion of patient access to cannabis products, particularly in underserved rural areas. There is also growing interest in broader cannabis reform, including the potential for recreational legalization in the future. However, given the state's conservative political climate, full adult-use legalization may take time.

Cannabis Culture in West Virginia's Major Cities

West Virginia's cannabis culture is still emerging, particularly in cities like Charleston, Morgantown, and Huntington, where medical cannabis dispensaries and CBD retailers are becoming more common. These cities are home to growing cannabis communities, with local patients, businesses, and advocates working together to promote the therapeutic uses of cannabis.

Charleston, as the state capital, has embraced the medical cannabis movement, with dispensaries offering patients access to a range of cannabis products. The city's focus on community health and wellness has made it a key location for medical cannabis reform in the state.

In Morgantown, cannabis culture is closely tied to the city's progressive attitudes and vibrant college community. Students and residents alike are increasingly turning to CBD products and medical cannabis as alternatives to traditional pharmaceuticals, helping to foster a supportive environment for cannabis reform.

Huntington, located along the Ohio River, has also seen growing interest in medical cannabis, with dispensaries offering patients relief from conditions like chronic pain and anxiety. Huntington's residents are active participants in the state's cannabis movement, and local businesses are contributing to the growth of West Virginia's cannabis market.

Cannabis Tourism in West Virginia

West Virginia's scenic beauty and outdoor recreational opportunities make it a potential destination for cannabis tourism, particularly as the state's medical cannabis program expands. Visitors to cities like Charleston and Morgantown can explore the state's growing CBD and wellness market, visiting CBD shops, wellness centers, and medical cannabis dispensaries.

While recreational cannabis is not yet legal in West Virginia, the state's focus on wellness tourism and natural remedies aligns with the goals of the medical cannabis program. Tourists visiting West Virginia can enjoy CBD-infused products and explore the state's natural beauty while learning more about the therapeutic benefits of cannabis.

Chapter 50: Hawaii - Cannabis and Wellness in Paradise

Hawaii, with its stunning landscapes and rich cultural traditions, has long been associated with wellness and natural health remedies. As one of the first states to legalize medical cannabis in 2000, Hawaii has embraced cannabis culture as part of its broader focus on health and wellness. Today, Hawaii's medical cannabis program continues to thrive, offering patients access to a variety of cannabis-based therapies, while the state explores opportunities for broader cannabis reform.

With its emphasis on holistic health, alternative medicine, and natural healing, Hawaii's cannabis industry is closely tied to the state's commitment to promoting wellness tourism. Visitors to Hawaii can experience the state's unique approach to cannabis and wellness, with dispensaries, wellness retreats, and cannabis-friendly events offering a range of cannabis-based experiences.

Hawaii's Medical Cannabis Program

Hawaii's medical cannabis program, established in 2000, was one of the first in the United States, reflecting the state's progressive attitudes toward natural medicine and alternative therapies. Under Hawaii's medical cannabis laws, patients with qualifying conditions, such as chronic pain, epilepsy, PTSD, cancer, and HIV/AIDS, can obtain a medical cannabis card with a physician's recommendation. The program allows patients to purchase cannabis products from licensed dispensaries and to grow their own cannabis for personal use.

Hawaii's medical marijuana program is overseen by the Hawaii Department of Health, which is responsible for licensing dispensaries and ensuring that cannabis products meet safety and quality standards. The state's dispensary scene is centered in cities like Honolulu, Maui, and Hilo, where patients have access to a variety of cannabis-based therapies, including flower, edibles, tinctures, and topicals.

Despite the success of Hawaii's medical cannabis program, there is growing interest in recreational legalization, particularly as the state continues to embrace wellness tourism. Advocates are pushing for legislation that would legalize adult-use cannabis, allowing Hawaii to tap into the potential of the recreational cannabis market while expanding access for patients and consumers alike.

Conclusion: The Future of Cannabis in the United States

As more states across the U.S. move toward cannabis legalization, the landscape of cannabis reform is changing rapidly. States like California, Colorado, and Oregon have paved the way for recreational cannabis, while others, like Missouri and Alabama, are leading the charge in medical cannabis reform.

The future of cannabis in the United States is bright, with economic opportunities, job creation, and patient access to therapeutic cannabis products continuing to drive the movement forward. As public opinion shifts and more states embrace cannabis legalization, the U.S. is on the path to a fully legal cannabis market, with the potential to transform industries and improve the lives of millions of Americans.

Made in the USA
Las Vegas, NV
22 November 2024

6999637b-1fe9-486e-9f9f-7d48e2cd50e5R02